Evelyn Araluen is a Goorie and Koori poet, editor and researcher. Born and raised on Dharug Country and in the broader Western Sydney Black community, she now lives on Wurundjeri Country where she is a lecturer at the Wilin Centre for Indigenous Arts and Cultural Development, a co-editor of *Overland Literary Journal* and Chairperson for the Board of the Institute of Postcolonial Studies. Her debut poetry collection, *Dropbear*, won the 2022 Stella Prize and the Australian Book Industry Award's 2022 Small Publisher's Adult Book of the Year, and was shortlisted for the premier's awards in New South Wales, Queensland and Victoria. Her work has also received the Nakata Brophy Prize for Young Indigenous Writers, the Judith Wright Poetry Prize and a Melbourne Prize Career Development Award.

Praise for *THE ROT*

'Evelyn Araluen's poetry and prose is created with a passionate intensity, razor-sharp intellect, beauty and compassion as she turns her mind to the broad sweep of history and a dynamic engagement with the spirit of our times.' **Alexis Wright**

'Rageful, desireful, artful, sorrowful, hauntful. A blaze of a book.' **Michelle de Kretser**

'Biting, anguished and revelatory.' **Melissa Lucashenko**

'Evelyn Araluen returns with a book of unblinking ferocity and corrosive beauty. She drapes her language across fractured hopes, decaying romances, forcing the reader into complicity with despair. But don't come here looking for epiphany, resolution or redemption. Araluen dismantles the idea that poetry should soothe or elevate, welding craft as rupture. *The Rot* is not to be read – it is to be reckoned with.' **Sara M Saleh**

'Blistering, brilliant, lacerating, wry, elegiac, *The Rot* is a hymn to girlhood, to resistance, to solidarity. Araluen is a masterful stylist, braiding air-fryer abjectioncore with bathtub meditations on the machinery of colonialism – and the whiplash and fury of witnessing and protesting genocide in the digital age. For all its allusions to mould and decay, *The Rot* is exhilarating in its defiance and staunchness.' **Jennifer Down**

'The "girlshaped thing" refuses manhandling in the rejection of imperial capital and the affirmation of those whose lives are unable to complete themselves because of colonial tyranny. It's a bookwork of wounds which refuses platitudes of repair. As capitalist militarism works to remove agency from the world, Evelyn Araluen rewrites the corrupt circuitry to insist on a poetics of justice. It seeks to staunch the flow of blood from wounds inflicted by global capital … This is a bookwork that shatters any preconceptions about "poetry and form" and "poetry and theme": the language morphs to avoid capitalist fetishisation and meaning becomes increasingly intricate as it arcs back to stark realities, absolute truths. An unforgettable journey that not only leaves its own marks of protest but clarifies the poison of archival erasure while questioning the manipulation by the state and capital of the archive itself, exposing the rot of empire. *The Rot* is a set of points we might move through and find a way to justice.' **John Kinsella**

Praise for *DROPBEAR*

'*Dropbear* is a breathtaking collection of poetry and short prose which arrests key icons of mainstream Australian culture and turns them inside out, with malice aforethought. Araluen's brilliance sizzles when she goes on the attack against the kitsch and the cuddly: against Australia's fantasy of its own racial and environmental innocence.' **Judges' comments, The Stella Prize**

'With subtlety and an occasional razor, Araluen interrogates colonial violence, conveys love of Country and family, and critiques the form itself, which has too often misrepresented Aboriginal people.' **Tony Birch**

'Evelyn Araluen dares to conjure old spectres, trope-busting her way through beloved Australian literary archetypes that still feed and sustain hallowed colonial fantasies and fixed-imaginings. This is an exquisite work of (un)reckoning and refusal where lessons and secrets reveal to unsettle and reclaim. A lasting imprint has been cast, storied with unnerving wit and wisdom and a heart so fierce and wide-open that we too love, pain, desire, and rupture through it all.' **Natalie Harkin**

'You know what to expect of a poet like Evelyn Araluen. Her verse has an unrivalled and merciless clarity of expression and purpose. In *Dropbear*, she peers through her subjects, right into you – the reader. Evelyn drops her words over gazes and shoulders like a heavy blanket – obscuring or warming, it's up to you.' **Alison Whittaker**

'Funny, savage and really insightful.' **Annabel Crabb, *Chat 10 Looks 3***

'[Araluen's] poetry, prose, and short form non-fiction meticulously unravels the myth-making of modern Australia. This work is a powerful act of sovereign resistance, breaking open the intersections of power, race and colonial fantasy. In this beautifully written and carefully constructed collection, she writes from her own embodied Black experiences offering the reader a demonstration of the power of the Black writer.' **Judges' comments, Victorian Premier's Literary Awards**

'*Dropbear* pushes genre boundaries and, more importantly, brings a rich intertextuality of entanglement – the messiness of the relationship between us and the history of the country that we can't change and shouldn't ignore.' **Jeanine Leane**

'The rigorous studies of language and colonial inheritance and political refusal in this collection are infused with a grace and ambition that wowed me. *Dropbear* acts as a testament of what has happened and what is yet to come. An important debut!' **Billy-Ray Belcourt**

'Superb … essential reading for anyone interested in "Australian" poetics or politics.' ***Books+Publishing***

'*Dropbear* is a living testimony to the power of words in the minds and hands of First Nations poets, activists and scholars as the works within this book speak beyond the surface to a deeper time and to bigger issues of unfinished business … a work of agency and radicalism.' ***Sydney Review of Books***

THE ROT

EVELYN ARALUEN

First published 2025 by University of Queensland Press
PO Box 6042, St Lucia, Queensland 4067 Australia
Reprinted 2026 (twice)

University of Queensland Press (UQP) acknowledges the Traditional Owners and their custodianship of the lands on which UQP operates. We pay our respects to their Ancestors and their descendants, who continue cultural and spiritual connections to Country. We recognise their valuable contributions to Australian and global society.

uqp.com.au
reception@uqp.com.au

Cover design by Jenna Lee
Typeset in 11/14 pt Adobe Garamond Pro by Post Pre-press Group, Brisbane
Printed in Australia by McPherson's Printing Group

University of Queensland Press is supported by the Queensland Government through Arts Queensland.

University of Queensland Press is assisted by the Australian Government through Creative Australia, its principal arts investment and advisory body.

A catalogue record for this book is available from the National Library of Australia.

ISBN 978 0 7022 6896 0 (pbk)
ISBN 978 0 7022 7043 7 (epdf)

University of Queensland Press uses papers that are natural, renewable and recyclable products made from wood grown in well-managed forests and other controlled sources. The logging and manufacturing processes conform to the environmental regulations of the country of origin.

For my girls, and the world you will make.

Anyone with pain.

Michael Ondaatje

CONTENTS

HOLDINGS

FRAGMENTS ON ROTTING

UNFOLDINGS

NOTES & ACKNOWLEDGEMENTS

HOLDINGS

Sleep Act One

The stars are leaving you.
In the city there's always light, sometimes
there's wind. The good wind holds you in
the doorway the first day it's warm enough
to bare your neck. A good wind bathes,
presses you into a room, makes you ask
the air before you can leave.
There are no bad winds, only dust and pollen
out of place, dragged through the lungs.
You have no business moralising what

you don't understand, like wind, city
planning, adaptive ecology. You get this way
when you stop sleeping. The world sits
offside just a little when you don't
break from it in years.
It is always light in the city, even in nights
flooded violet with melatonin, wine in
the bath, a cup of sleepy tea, a few licks of
your lover's seroquel, ibuprofen for
the aches, retinol for the lines, three
days deep sobbing to the wikipedia entry
for pigeons, theatres of hygiene and
fascism in alternating screens, *I will never*
forgive you if you do not share this video,
a full basket you will never check out,
muting notifications for the groupchat
so you won't stumble on a new grief
to impale your dreams. There is light but
no breeze, there is night but no sleep,
the fire map tells you the place you can't
call home without footnotes has a low
halo of smoke drifting through wattle.
You imagine it blurring stars as
they scatter to the furthest horizon from
your undeserving reach.
We are all slouching towards the bearable
living, turning backs to the violent edge.
You are missing sleep, there is
too much time left, too much
of that vengeful wind, that light that
needs you not to look
away.

Invocations

On reading Brontë, on reading Rankine,
on reading di Prima read Marx
and listening to Fisher explain that
those who can't remember the past are
condemned to have it sold to them forever,
then rewatching again that scene where
the dead friend says she will take
the displaced surplus of love that
grief leaves for us to swallow for herself,
the room a tender glow of steampunk LEDs
you bought from the crude oil store
with money you were paid for poems
howling to the dead,
on spilling fake wine over every restless vital
urgent document you're yet to read,

on the citational praxis of begging him
to stay in this world forever,
on and against the commonwealth,
in and without the bloodiness of language
hidden in books they never wanted
the dirty hording masses to read,
on the power of states to misremember us
how we learnt of the things that kill them,
on the black cockatoos rising
from the still-swamped scrub
and the radiant hum of the screen
as your lofi-beats-to-study-to wife
turns her gaze to the moon,
on her place also against the wall
as we condemn those who attempt
to resell us peace forever,
on the things we gave to the fire
and what was owed to the flood,
on the earnt necessity of revolution
as the only way we have to forgive ourselves,
on the ghosts we have disappointed and
now the haunting that is the only
thing left to do,
burning like evening light through
bare branches of trees that don't
belong in this land,
on the arrangement of electricity it
takes to memorialise them,
against the dead centre
of this work,
and the names you swore
to take with you.

Billionaire Liturgy

how to make a billion? incubate god in a crypto mine and
never leave an orangutan in one piece – the supply chain
connects to the kill chain, places every flailing wire in
your hands

who could ever know how much a billion costs?
the weight of oceans, rates of miscarriage,
coal forests collapsing into desert

does a billion still feel lonely when it splutters from the
LLM, prompt propulsion mining stars from the dirt?

for a billion you'll need a billion
bones of a billion small birds, a billion
shimmering fish, a billion crimes, a billion
incandescent bribes for the cops, you could
feed a billion to the dopamine machine
and never touch the sides, he'll spit you
out a deportation compound, the code to
automate the domicide protocol, before
you know it you'll be communing with
The Market in faster-than-real-time

there's big business in privatising the clocks, in bottling air,
offer it up to the deities of the dow jones nasdaq s&p 500
temple complex, praise be the discount code for kettling,
praise be the mercy of kings

do billionaires dream of a billion sheep?
do they dream of the day they can say *honey, the kids*
are home, honey, they've forgiven us?

a billion young
to buy back with
lifestyle subsidy convenience
something to take your mind
off all that horror hovering six
inches from your face

where do you bury a billion?
if you gave them three wishes
they'd wish for a billion more

always more buyers for new blood
a billion machines to make and kill desire
a billion hours of sleep to buy back

what's the formula to make a billion? a billion
eel runs, emu nestings, gathering days, a billion ways
to make the trains leave on time

call it collateral damage
call it empire call it
back from whence it
came and salt the fucking
grounds

is a billion still a billion in space? up there
are we as small as a billion leaves
shimmering from a billion trees?

how far will you fly to
forget a billion souls? how far do you
have to be from the gun and the
knife before the recoil won't shudder
in your hand? before the blood
won't touch your face?

Real Estate

The best minds of our generation are
sourcing rent from mutual aid, are

inhaling mould knowing there
will be no old age to pay it back.

These are things we can't talk about
with the windows open. Fuck the

email candour, *you'd better hope this one*
finds you before I do. Our house

slants on its stumps and holds heat
like a toothache throbbing the night.

Run your tongue across the walls, if
we can't afford our living at least

we can spoil it with our spit. It's all
rock'n'roll baby, the way packing

boxes set a dust in your hands that won't
move til you do. Being still a little young,

you get angry when you remember any time
you didn't fight back, at the service fee

for the robot working your old job.
No-one ever hurt you in these rooms

you didn't invite in yourself. The moths
the damp the harpy the real estate,

all these ghouls chewing on your
flesh and hair.

Your ancestors lived on the river
the stations the mines

and now you owe the air
another debtor's weight in gold.

Whatever time is left was
ransomed from drowning islands in

the Pacific, so fuck the baseboards
and the lawn, just leave the teeth marks

on the wrist and remember
where to scrub next time.

You are angry at your emails
at the sum of human history

at the open sewer they left in
your yard for a month and

the wind flinging pollen in your eyes.
Everything you could buy to chemical

sleep from the draft inflates
some cunt's shareholder value.

You're writing poems on bullets, taking
names and addresses, no you will

not be getting your bond back, no
there are no pets on the premises.

Bonney said if we're not burning cop cars
we're nowhere, then the algo

tried to sell you Hello Kitty mace.
The science says we are

running out of sand, that the
US has misplaced six nuclear bombs,

and we have eaten the sea almost empty. You
will never be who you were before Gaza,

you think of home every night you lay down
in this quiet gentle place you forget you'll have

to leave, you forget you cannot keep.
It's not always bad, even in the city you sometimes

hear old ngarehr splitting the sky. If you
were less hungry this might be enough—

this ancient song, an apology from god.
You hear the landlord is lovely, you think of her when

the roses bite your sleeve.

Upfield Line

you old dog you / you sardine huddled in the tin you /
you sardine tin jostling in a La Manna shopping basket
brimming with other assorted tins / all dressed beautiful
adorned citrus fragrant earthy spice staining the glossy oil
that seeps through a canvas tote like you won't believe /
you with your shuttering vistas warehouses car park artists
residencies luxury co-dwelling homing startups co-looming
over weathered weatherboard workers cottages / they
thems reading a Ferrante they started at Kines before
knock-offs at Flippys, those stupid European cups / pepper
trees heaving chain-link fences / gotta keep the trains in
their crates lest they grow restless and destructive / like a
shivering greyhound biochemically engineered to hunt and
slaughter teacup cavoodles with deathly precision / once
a wolf, behold Custard, gemini rising, trembling in socks
and a Labubu dangling from an anxiety vest, nipping at the

customers lingering outside A1 / Upfield Line service dead zones contracted by Merri-bek Labor hacks to intercept your screen time / Royal Park arranging a daily dose of unbouquetted flora has you squinting, like this could all be almost bearable if you don't mind the airborne golf-ball risk / *fuck golf, turf and terfs alike, amirite?* you think of flirting to your train girlfriend, think of her turning her face back to the window, indifferent unamused in her crochet bonnet / think of watching her vaping at 7.55am her mullet haloed by blue raspberry plume, the most beautiful thing you've never spoken to this side of Sydney Road / Upfield Line a stuttering fluorescent beam above the deli counter, radiating over heaving shelves of salted baccalà and limbs of sopressa as big as the geometric toddlers squealing and scattering the debris of an $18 báhn mì / Upfield Line a shimmering door between two unyielding rooms / a comfy commute for the comfortable / a live-action working-class extraction machine / decompress your seasonal depression with a tour of the desaturated federation double-front industrial complex / returning from the Upfield Line your neighbour soliloquises how much these streets have changed since he bought his place for $40k and drove a Cadillac in the Keating administration / above you the ringtails are scrambling to assemble new dreys after the council workers fold down the tree crane / you want to say that you too know what it is to lose a temporary world / instead you compliment the roses, commiserate on the frozen dawn ahead / go home to a home you can't afford and pack your lunch box for your lunch tote for the lunch hour of the workday already grinding the soles of your boots / another night another morning another train on the Upfield Line / you door you, you promise of a life you couldn't live if you wanted to /

Blood Wash

girls, what are we buying
to soak up all this blood?
constellation points
of the abject
video essay
industrial complex
mucous membrane
redemption arc
how pretty you
are the anaemic glow
always
eleven, horrified
betrayed
picking hardened
lumps of blood
from hair
don't forget
to situate
biblical analogies
the recuperative slasher
neoliberal mobile capital
send your boyfriend
to the chemist
did you learn that
on the back of a pad?
meanwhile
chunks clotting over
the shower drain
meanwhile a highway
splitting birthing

trees meanwhile
in gaza girls bleed
on tent scraps sliced by
bunker busters
christened by white
phosphorus
over 85,000 tons of
imperial commodity
always a ■■■
ready
teething at the bit
the pain is
normal the pain is not
even there
the oldest story
actually you are angry
you are hysterical
your wandering womb
redshift eclipsing
the latest genre of
gender fetish
a cup a pill a vapour
a labour a
metal stench
have you tried aesthetic
rehabilitation?
have you tried
dragging this across
the desert to repent?
have you tried
something more
to not afford?
haven't you noticed
girls do be girling

so much these days?
haven't you noticed
so much is in your name?
actually you are angry
all that shaving
all the starving
katy perry burning
carbon for the culture
self-anointing martyrs
of toilets and
storytimes never
girls girls for the girls
that never get home
forgetting
the bricks the
coathangers
it took
and meanwhile
and actually
you are
you are angry
bloody hysterical
how couldn't you be?
old wounds
always
opening and
closing and
oozing all
around
remember that's
the point
it takes a player to etc.
the game was getting you
used to blood

Girl Work!

good morning, girly! the sun is bright
and east in your eyes that freezing wind
from someplace bullshit
icing off your liner
you've got affirmations to rehearse
to the backing vocals of a doomsday podcast
indexing our crimes against the earth

girly, you glisten in your soft tailoring
wide-leg sambas boxy-blazer co-ord
your coolgirl cleangirl chic
that pulled back pony at the root point
of your embodiment
your anchor against this season's aporia

it's a fine day to disassemble
to the first page of a fractal anti-femmemoir
on your way to commune with the machine
to take a meeting
that could have been a bullet

wake up, babe, they killed god
and you can watch it back
on your second screen

girly, are you on?
you're already two rem cycles behind
you haven't had a feeling since they
banned lime scooters from the city

the latest shipment of micro-aggro
extractions just landed and
we need someone to macro-manage
quality control in the holocene
we need something to keep our
lives beautifully organised
and we think you've got that
tabi-toe structure for the job

o girly, ain't it so divine?
ever since you were a little thing
you wanted screen time and iced coffee for breakfast
to nudge a cursor and collect a work
wage to afford cute outfits for work
for a place to stay when you're not working
to save for a holiday from work

girly, there's something rotten in your keep cup
and you're always at risk of an early lunch
girlboss, you just need another public holiday
just some bog time and a cigarette

o girly, lift your head! it's not so bad
in this shining new era of girlgods
it's your choice to girlsleep girlwoke girlcope
they'll remind you later that your institution
is forcing an update
the dreams you buried are
indexed against your life on loan

girly, are you losing the way? o, all
your sardonic laconic slants

the hottest superwaif to ever ache
at the function
girly, it's so chic to neither fuck
nor be fucked
to abstract all stakes in your living
to swallow the rot and your profit on it

girly, it's all for the plot
for the prettiest pigeons swarming in the streets
mao said imperialism is ferocious and
fuck me dead don't you feel that one in your tits

o girly, it's not even all your fault
who has leisure time for revolution these days?
you're too busy stacking hours
at the reconciliation factory
got too many sex pests in the union anyway
some days you don't know if you're a body
or just a breakout bubbling beneath the skin

o girly,
who amongst us has not been shaken by the
last spluttered breaths of the machine?
our mama the internet
our papa the technocratic state
o girly, who has time to remember?
whose job is it to tell you
how small
you are?

Sleep Act Two

You don't dream of labour or
electric sheep, just the darkest
shapes before dawn.
This is what you've learnt to
keep from the moon—
sentiment, regret, scorpions
pacing the doorframe or the
blade upturned on the rug. This
one is a floor plan you move
through overheated to leave a room
vibrating with conversations
you can't translate. Sleep bleeds gasoline,
night is a wire you left hitched
to the back of the car. Today you
learnt the shape of the microplastics
swirling and snowglobing in your skull—
the toll your body has been charged
for living under capital is the weight
of a spoon. You don't know how many
throats of asbestos it took

to kill your grandparents or
how much lead is in your mother, but
still, it would be less than the bullets
in the mass graves of Gaza. Hind
begged for her life for three hours.
Again. Hind begged for her life for
three hours. Again. Hind begged for
her life for three hours. No poem
can say more than this. Say that Hind
begged for her life for three hours,
commit it to history that Israel has gone
unchecked for genocide, then *pick up a stone,*
there are children in the street.
It's not you or yours that trade in
ruins. You'll go home when you die to
live a different way. But you are here
now and have hands, fists. When your
dreams hold these truths in their clear
light the spoon tries to mix them back
together. A shareholder decides our brains
are best kept liquid, that the firmness
of the world might tempt us to change.
If we hoard the tiny plates and plastic
spoons perhaps they'll miss
the knives, the pitchforks. Keep them
on a hard drive you can hide from
the moon, make copies
in books the cops can't read.
Store what you can in resin,
make sure not to swallow the dust.
When they try to tell you a different
story, tell this one over and over again.

Retired from sad new career in geese

There's always a screen somewhere
telecasting a promised life against a wall.

Someone calls your name as if for the first time,
there is bread in the kitchen and desire
summons you to a river where you are loved for
strangeness and wry.

We can't all be on our way to a party.
Too much heat and fray,
disaster nationalism and radiant tragedy
to fill the nights. There's no purpose
walking west til your feet have lightened,
no horizon free and safe for the girls.
If they could invent a place
where you belong, you'd
mistake the door and claim your
kingdom on the lawn.

This didn't need to be an elegy.
Most of life is making love work,
clearing space on the counter, folding
back the things we've learnt to
endure. Don't let me down again,
you beg the cobwebs assembling the
dew. We all have histories we forget
are still strapped to our backs, your
mother is always trying in her broken
ways to tell you what was done to her.

Go ask the rhizome what it's about,
the radial project, finding somewhere safe
to hold your splinter of the moon.
Nothing will appease your
need to know
what happens next, not even
the certainty it will be worse. But
still, please, you say. Your hand in mine
another moment, just a little more, still.

Every day we are rescued by whims and
fancy, the breeze from the sea. If there's
more to be had, we should have invested
from the womb. You repeat the argument
every few months, he remembers a shriek,
you still feel the wail. The geese aren't
coming to save us this time, Mary, they're
out there swimming in the cold stars. It will
always have been worth it, we need to
believe. But, please, you will say, give me
just a moment, just another moment more.

You

return here to pace the dream where your
strangeness couldn't protect you from the
wound. This winter it will be different, a new
blanket heavy enough to hold you down, another
augury to find in the storm. Neither weep
nor abstain. Between the sorrow and the horror
we chose grief, the species loneliness of magnolias,
the last satellite blind in the dark. Home, the dawn,
a night no-one can take back, your bones hungering
for the soil. All your longing is yours, no matter
what you're told. If we'd known we'd get here
we couldn't have, if we'd explained, we would have
lost you from the only place we have to call hope.
Rest a moment. Remember who you shared the
earth with, what joined your depths of darkness and joy.
There are teeth marks and a train window in us all.
There are finches that sing in their sleep. Make you
no less human than yourself. Around us the
world sways, sometimes crumbles. It's not that
you think you can change this, but you need
something to do with your hands.

FRAGMENTS ON ROTTING

decay, putrefaction
decline in function and or appearance
decomposition in the citadel of life
disease: moral, social, natural
also, degeneration: moral, social, political
corrosion, rust, dissolution
a wound, the old story,
the body the state the earth in spoil
the ruin the rudus
what's left before
there's nothing left

till we be roten
kan we nat be ripen

(i) 256GB OF SALVAGED MEMORY

In a scene you remember as if it were your own life, a girl scribbles her longings and days in the margins of a book written in languages she cannot read. She rises from her perch in the rubble to return to a shelf exposed to the moon and rain while the walls of the library crumble into the hillside and exposed horizon. Figures move in the periphery of rooms adjusted to wounds of war, of time. Somewhere in the exposed organs of the house someone is dying.

You summon here by bookmark every time you restart the machine, a window that never closes, a path grown over in the organic infrastructure of memory. For most of your life you've been tending this archive. In corroded folders and pixel halo you call up the bones of your yearnings and fixations, fragments of consciousness, notes tracing your entrance and maintenance in a symbolic order of being, both more and less of gender, desire, history. No matter where you roam she is there, set in the closed books on the shelf. The wind lifts from the sea, calcifies the pages, rot sets in at the spine. Sometimes you pry them out for display, as if to offer your naked throat, the back of your fermented tongue.

Revisiting yourself you sift tidemarks, stuttered triptychs, the bildungs and translation-loss of shadows, the burnt bulb of the hyperlink or lapses in cell typography, contemplate whether it was the dust-risen ray of yellow light striking a newly weathered photograph or the unopened door in a hallway. Lithograph, eucalypt silhouette, kohl stain under the eye, a dead actress begging shadows, the perpetual palimpsest calling *unend me / shipwreck me / bullfight me / I am your / war to word /* sepia face glitching on the sudden prophetic, emulsions of decaying light colouring lurid spectres you think you felt there all along. *THE YOUNG-GIRL SIGNIFIES AN IMPATIENT RAGE TO ABOLISH MATTER AND TIME / SHE IS A BODY WITHOUT SOUL DREAMING SHE'S A SOUL WITHOUT A BODY.* An empty bed, a clavicle, a rib, a cavern of thigh. The pattern announces itself even in its broken code: what are you looking for in this body? Can you make it small enough to pass through the eye? Dead cells blink back, another life you sowed not to reap.

Long nights looming in the holiness of kept things. The folk aetiology of a dying star, all helium and sparks in the void. You return every little while with a prayer, a burial. The window glass exploding shards through the aisle, the links rotted out, the playlist grinning tooth evulsion, win32 deletion litany spreading through your shoulder, your spine, your femoral artery.

The pattern announces itself again, again: who did you trust to do your remembering for you? What will it cost to claw you back?

Terms of Reference

(i) The designs of woman you are proscribed through empire fix on the mark of █████ as its oppositional yet constitutive force. What you have known as 'woman', 'girl', 'daughter', 'sister', 'mother', 'girlfriend', 'wife', 'whore', 'slut', 'bitch', 'gin', 'lubra' is tethered by relationality in the mode of address – a familial, romantic, subordinate, derisive or colonial bearing.

(ii) Under empire, you are legible by your subjugation under the state's repressive and reproductive powers. *You* as function of *It* both constituted and eclipsed by history, something womanshaped to be salvaged by feminism or psychoanalysis or dialectical materialism, always bound at the ankles, the shifting legislature of the state. Your trauma, your negation, the only mark of you as object that holds in the narrative, transcribed as consequence of biology or occupation.

(iii) How much of this is to find a way to say that she died the day the boats came? That a body already dead can only ever be a ghost?

(iv) A flinch, a compulsive rejoinder. What you are that is not legible under empire is not in a here that can be looked in the eye, is not evocable by these stories and does not stir for those words, is perhaps still washing in the river in Baryulgil, wandering the hills of Molong, is resting on the banks of the Dyarubbin or waits in the lonely dark at Dennewan. There are threads of your mother sewed into the quilt she made for your wedding bed, or perhaps they are still in the aches and calluses of her hands.

(v) The girlshaped thing cannot escape that set of mouths against her neck, that which has made you feel most her gender: what has been done to you by ■■■, and what you have consumed in the always at-once project of becoming and unbecoming woman.

(vi) This is your lens. You hold a mirror in your hand where the bodies drift in and out, texts, affect, commodities, the wind. Each point of relation rearranges itself on a screen while you organise your spectres.

(vii) Your instincts are yours but you did not choose them, they hover in the air where you watched it happen to her, saw what it took from the rest of your days.

(viii) She is there, and you are somewhere, and somewhen.

(ix) Also, and again, again, and again.

i. hip

That old wound again, dull amber familiar pain, radiant from
the femoral head to acetabulum, those bones crushed back
to the joint a generation ago, hobbling beside your father,
that street stretched from the haunted house to the cemetery
at the foot of the old rollerblade rink,

never again,

the mutter leaving the chiropractor, the duskbird
calling a circling ache for your nights.

It'll always be here, don't you know? That memory lives in
your hip, down at South Windsor shops, in every doctor's
office and in the centre cavern of your too-soft mattress.
You insisted on it when so briefly flush with cash, you feel it
pulling on your spine's small – lumbar, sacrum – stony ache
and arms waking dead under the pillow.

At ten you were told belly
sleeping would flatten your tummy.

What drags you to a sinking centre also withholds sleep, has
forbidden rolling over or the taking of anti-inflammatories
for the ache or antihistamines for the rotting carpet fibres
in your nose or melatonin for the dream. In day you cannot
delay dinner to stretch or see a doctor or answer emails.
You are condemned to stillness and pain in the dark,
you are a lucid bruise in the night.

In the house on the corner there's a figure in a blood-soaked
surgeon's coat performing night-time operations on the hips
of young girls. In your uncle's back paddock a crow is rising
from the earth, his gleaming wings unfolding as he flays the
scalp from the skull. You are walking the street with your
lover and the piano falls, there is only time for them to beg
you to claw their ribs back together but you are stone and
still for the rest of your years without them. Around you the
house is burning and all the ancient pollinators of the world
are turning to dust.

The notifications hum and glow stage directions
you won't find in the morning:

the ████ who hurt you when you
were fifteen hurts you the same way
as the ████ who hurt you when you
were twenty-one, but he has the face
of the boy you loved at nineteen, and
it is your fault,
your fault because you did not
save the girl who asked for
your help when you were twelve.

Most nights you are girlshaped following the slow revolution of stars under the window to that green side passage your sister used for her escapes, feet crunching gravel, those old cockatoo fires curving the sky. Some nights are stuck behind the chook pen watching yourself in the dark, in the brown caravan under the macadamia tree or tracing the edge of the dam while plovers screech the moon's creased reflection.

The grounds you don't sleep are plentiful and glimmer in their memories of you. Against their shadows you practise new catastrophes in the dark. Eyes open or closed to the shapes clawing out of corners, strangers pacing outside the door, the snakes writhing the gutters.

You are here in a resting hollow for heavy histories with deep
grooves to grind and old feuds to bury. Your nights are
holding ground for something out of place,
passing through.

No matter. No stars for belly
sleepers. No sleep for them
that bruise the world.

(ii) 256GB OF SALVAGED MEMORY

1. Doorways, halls, windowframes, landings and aisles photographed in every angle.

2. The saddest song in the world on repeat.

3. At least a dozen still lifes of fruit in varying stages of decay.

4. Bees piously assembling their honeycomb cells around icons of the crucified Christ.

5. The crusted scab you peel back in perpetuity.

6. Typewritten notes on exposure therapy administered by strangers unqualified to offer medical advice.

7. A hundred collages of ruderal species, time lapses of nettle and vine splitting concrete, rusted machines fossilising into ancient forests, knotweed protruding radiant from the fallout zone.

8. Eighteen gifs of Stevie Nicks haunting
Lindsey Buckingham.

9. A plaintive shadow of a hand on a wall, a pollen bruise on a knee.

10. Aggressively decontextualised fragments of Sontag, Plath, Carson, Angelou.

11. A view to a sunwashed city. A cup of water, a lavender sprig on the sill. No flyscreen, no scorpions, no lords, no masters.

12. Moors, heath, rubble, the red flush of desire on the porcelain skin of girls who never look like you.

13. That damned line about Brooklyn that won't stop scraping your throat.

14. A forty-five-minute supercut of the pursuing lover collapsing at the feet of the resistant lover, preferably wailing as they crush their face against the lower belly and pubic bone.

15. Approximately three hundred saved videos of lower-belly exercises.

16. A four-hour compilation of Coppola girls doing their hair and makeup.

17. A six-hour montage of women crying in mirrors, 35mm.

18. Spears of oversaturated windowlight falling on artfully crumpled sheets.

19. Mitski howling into her guitar, *Mum, can you wash my back this once, and then we can forget?*

20. An apology still marked by the indents of your clenched jaw.

21. Faded underlines and dog-eared corners shortcutting back to the ghosts and darlings you'll never kill.

22. A smudge of handwriting across the margin: *how much longer?*

23. The same nothing you can't stop coming back for.

On Desire

(x) *Desire is involved with the not yet and, at times, the not anymore*, writes Unangax̂ philosopher Eve Tuck. Desire here is a refusal of imperial deficit and colonial damage, as an hauntological mode of inhabiting the archive with embodied practices to affirm the sovereignty of land and spirit.

(x) When you were a little girl you imagined desire as the answer to grief: the lover who longs for his departed, spectral almost-bride. Eros unconsummated, fermenting in perpetual mourning, a melancholia so potent it mists the moors and brings the ghost to the glass.

(x) You return to this fixation because you've been thinking about dying, of the way girls and women die.

(x) Tuck's sense of desire builds from Jameson's aphorism that *History is what hurts. It is what refuses desire and sets inexorable limits to individual as well as collective praxis*. Across several essays Tuck and her collaborators interrogate the denying and dominating function of settler-colonial knowledge institutions such as universities, galleries and museums, and the limitations they set on those who are Othered by those spaces. The absorption of Aboriginal subjectivity into the settler-colonial archive is structured by the privileging of academic knowledge, by institutions always positioning themselves as universal and objective. The academy, the museum, the archive, the comment section: all affirmations of capitalist and colonial narratives of deficit, of damage.

(x) What you are told you are or were once is there, suspended luminescent in formaldehyde.

(x) Desire, for Jameson, moves counterlogical to the history that hurts: desire is how we speak to the stories and praxes that were never recognised by history, or were intentionally erased.

(x) For Tuck and Yang, desire *invites the ghosts that history wants exorcised, and compels us to imagine the possible in what was written as impossible.* In this sense, they write, *desire is haunted.*

(x) This tells you, desire is not the reconstitution of historical narratives in their time and place, but the summoning of spectres into the present from which we remember and remind of them.

(x) This tells you, you found it easier to imagine yourself a dead girl desired than a living woman loved.

i. Long Future

You were slouching towards something, always biting the inside of your mouth. July 2015, Tuck:

How we shall live is the driving question of my concerns with theories of change, she says, and around you a before and after assembles. *The need for justice may outlast my years, and I have children in this world. I am a mother and I need time to bathe my children, to care for them and help them grow.*

Before, after, within.

We are all fractured by the knotted claims of time. The before hinged by these words was a stumbled limping thing, floating aimlessly through a PhD you didn't remember starting, little more than anxiety to show for your labours. The work, if there was work, had long since lost shape and purpose. You carried a portable hard drive in your bag full of Marxist readings you didn't understand, you wore a full face of makeup to the gym. You struggled to read so instead watched video essays and recorded lectures, collecting notes on your phone as you drifted between rallies, bushcare, language classes and the library. People you had called your friends claimed they feared you, your anger, your resentment. You were unwell then, not in the way they wanted to imagine, not in the way you had been before or would later become, and not in the way you are now.

You were stagnant and already falling over your too-quickly-growing-feet. Then Nan died and your nocturnal months began. Then you forgot the muscle memory that disordered your eating for you, the easiness of hanging skin off bone. Then your cleverness stopped outstripping your lack of discipline and decided it would be better spent whispering all your wrongs through the night. Then the dawn, then the day, then the dusk. You never asked yourself how you would live, you just woke one day too old for someone to tell you.

When you could finally accept that research on Indigenous cultures is more often a project of reinscribing deficit, a before and after emerged in you that returned your feet to the soil. Research can also be invasion, Tuck reminded you, can fetishise our pain and violation, can make us believe the only thing you can do with a wound is tell it, can make us forget what we want. When we choose to hold our power within our worlds, we refuse the axiom that research is the only intervention needed, we remind ourselves that there are forms of knowing the academy does not deserve.

These challenges to the damage stories that had been dragging at your ankles held root in what was always already within you. You finally saw the birthing grounds of an idea. You knew it in the bone-deep intimacy of familial care, of reproductive labour, of Indigenous lifeways of persevering against historical orders demanding our erasure. Synapses lit up in your brain and you could recall the rooms where you read about the abstractions these words made legible. Tuck charted this genealogy of inquiry so you could map the connective tissues that bind her to these questions – through Muscogee scholar Daniel Wildcat, through Oglala Lakota historian Vine Deloria Jr, through the grief of burying family, the loss of mentors – you could feel through your fingers that the question of how we shall live alongside our need for justice is communal, a realisation of the shared worlds we must believe we will continue to inhabit together, of the shared risks we must accept for their reckoning.

Tuck's conviction is rooted in what she calls the *long future*: the time we will have after colonisation has ended, the things that will remain or return that have always been here, and will be here again. Part praxis, part hope, the long future is a promise to outlive the colony and to restore what was taken from the world to build it. You see its trace in what Tuscarora writer Alicia Elliott means when she says *things that were stolen once can be stolen back* – the collective condolence ceremony that will guide us to see the beauty of our own ways again.

For once you held an idea that didn't dissolve when you turned from the screen. You gave your knowing blood by telling your father what you thought it all meant when you drove to bushcare on the weekend, bouncing across the cab while he edged around branches brought up from the last flood. You told him, effective negation depends on the specificity of the object. If we are to recognise what's missing, we first need to know its shape, how it looks in the light and in the dark. Settlement cannot be wished away, the past cannot be altered by wishing it, there are still long shadows reaching over the land. As such, you insisted, our work, like that of other mob who walk before and alongside us, is to wade through the detritus of history if we want to survive it.

And he liked it, in most ways he already knew it, so he came back next week with another handful of pages he wrote instead of sleeping.

ii. Long Future

1. Get a few weeks of decent sleep.

2. Go to the library, take your tablets.

3. Linger and levitate through the debris of every room you haunt, the shrapnel casings of scribbled pages, a naked branch shaking off decaying post-its that scatter across the sunken wreck of journals each only five pages full, a paper carcass inhaling and exhaling above a calcified laptop vibrating with weeks of sixteen open word docs.

4. Take the instinct and muscle memory of your bush wandering into the digital world. Loop back to check your blind spots. Collect every scrap of every adaptation of you, forsake version control, endlessly repeat your longings and fixations through archives of unread terms of service, buy it back by subscription, factory reset to the last girl's algorithm just for the comfort of a place you've been before.

5. Never answer an email promptly, never complete a request, never forgive yourself for your failure to thrive.

6. Get up, put on a load of washing, research financial eschatology and the warning signs of a cyclone.

7. Press yourself unmoored and unready into dealings that wound, that fracture agency and show your enemies where it hurts most. When your cardinal points drag you to learnings made long before you came to this side of the earth, splutter, gasp, barely find your breath, barely listen before you fling yourself against the sea again.

8. Act as if you believed in an alchemy of intellectual and creative productivity that can displace hands on the earth. Convince yourself that work is the antidote to despair.

9. Tell yourself you're building a toolkit to disrupt the extractive logics of colonial research: theories of change, refusal, desire, suspending damage. Tangle yourself in citation, methodology, abstraction, antinomy. Buy and trade in half-remembered footnotes, forget where you left that long future and the work we must do to live in it. Never read past the introduction. Open but do not enter every door you stumble past.

10. Rewrite the line in your memory, tell yourself it was always about brushing hair, watching children warm by the fire. See only the place of labour in domesticity and the domesticity in care.

11. Refuse to forgive your mother for her mother. Refuse to see why she anoints the damned.

12. Take the dog to the park and pour a glass of wine for the bath just to lose the day, the work with it. Disintegrate into the steam that rots the walls.

13. Displace your foreboding, the sense that worse days are already on their way. Dissociate in the stories of every land but your own while grasping handfuls of wattle and running fingers along barbed wire. Test the outline of the poems you might write if you could ever kill the cento in your head.

14. Remember how your friend said in their long future there would be time to read everything and to look after their mates when they're sick.

15. Tie yourself back to the muscle when you can, to the scar tissue when you can't. To Moreton-Robinson and resistance, to Said and storytelling, to Fanon and re-narration, to Glissant and opacity. To the old stories of the moon and the dew.

16. Slowly and stumblingly let it sit in the room with you, what you can't name, what you can't summon back.

17. Take long walks along the edge of the reserve at the golden hour and think of the strategic advantage of taking the money and running into the horizon.

18. Weave through creekwater-stained tea-tree, blossoming and burning scrub, the sun sliced sideways as scribbled skin soaks and cracks in the heat of firestorms we could have stopped if we were only allowed.

19. Write that walk over and over again, not knowing how soon you would leave it.

20. Trace endlessly around the tenor of resistance, the thing that once you had known it was all for: our land, and the lives we deserve to live there.

21. Say it now, but never then. This was always meant to hurt.

iii. Long Future

One day you will post a clip from the lecture that rewired your brain and gave you a hand to hold through the frailty of your own visions, the same clip you shared with your sister that gave her the language to articulate her grief and helped your students put words to their rage, and a white anarchist in your DMs will tell you that Tuck married a cop. You know this accusation is meant for you.

ii. hip

That dream again, or is it? You are ten and your walking has become a problem. Your mother works two jobs, your father is taking your sister to the specialist again. How to keep a wandering girlshaped thing who reads of moors and brambles from the bush, the paddocks, the wrens murmuring in the undergrowth, horses kicking dust along the fenceline at the back of dirtbike city, all those staging grounds for the old stories, all that theatre so hungry for the open sky?

Once you saw a stormdrain full of marbles, a white bull on the dam's island, a gunshot in the air. The dark stallion rears up along the path, a hound roars through the mist. Cars slow beside you and you have learnt not to turn your head, to avoid the eyes of spirits and ■■■. Their voices lean from the open window, you live on that farm up the road? You saw a dog round here? Where's ya mum at, darl?

You're there for the birds, the suncracked clay, the only horizon with room enough for your dreaming. Your hip aches if you don't walk enough. Already you are thinking of your body, of what you must do to make it smaller. You don't speak, sometimes you run. Sometimes you are fast enough.

i. On Ghosts

1. While death holds the gaze of the ███, a girl is never presumed to look it in the eye. Death looms in all versions of female escape we allow ourselves, romantically evaporating at the boundary stone, hovering at the limit of the prospect, guiding the ley line that runs beneath the territory wall and catches spirits in the whins and brambles. Death stains the sheets, pools at the feet, makes solitude a currency, a gamble.

2. The death of young girls in literature and culture fixates, is charged with erotic spectre:

    a. Doyl says *we would rather see girls stopped dead – stuck in a constant childhood that never decays – than let them grow into women who can pursue their desires.*

    b. Chang says *godhood is just like girlhood: a begging to be believed.*

    c. Guest says *I'm not sure when this rage came to be. If I was born with it inside of me, if it grew alongside me all these years.*

3. Under this regime of her iterability, the girl is born already a ghost. In dying, she sheds an earthly vessel already risking decomposition, autonomy.

4. The girlshaped thing resumes her work as a god. Untouchable, irretrievable, forever already somewhere else.

ii. On Ghosts

Scenes deleted from Cary Joji Fukunaga's 2011 adaptation of *Jane Eyre* open on misted moors and the spectral figure of Helen Burns beckoning to Jane, her childhood companion. Exhausted, alone and betrayed, Jane stumbles to her across the grass and stone before collapsing soporose in the heath. They are together again, just as they had once lain as girls in the chapel, each on another side of living. Helen's hand gently caresses Jane's while the open sky moves above, tangling strands of their hair in the wind.

Through this gaze we are called to this story by Helen, who always fantasised of her own departure to the kingdom of heaven. Helen waiting in a frozen girlhood all these years to bring her friend to a dreamworld imagined to withstand beatings, starvation, exposure, and finally the consumptive illness that took the lives of so many at Lowood School.

We wonder if Helen has been lonely in her afterlife, the only place she had to call home.

In this telling of the story, Helen's silent, sullen spectre lingers in the corners, doorways and mirrors of Thornfield Hall, a dreamy double to the Grey Lady of old country houses feared by Rochester's guests, and a quiet guard against the vengeful attic wife who rummages through the hope chest and sets fire to the beds. Helen sits with Jane as she plans her escape from the house while Rochester howls from behind the door. Helen shows Jane that the house of a ████ married to a ghost can only be left through windows.

Out there in a world that has proven itself cold and unyielding to those without means or connection, only the heather will embrace the girls.

This withheld story strains the same nets that dragged the Brontë sisters to their premature deaths. At the juncture of a cold and cruel Calvinist father and the heavydeep spirits looming the Yorkshire moors, through Helen, Charlotte offers us the only righteous death for a girl.

Liberated from the cumbrous frame of flesh, Helen, siren of the afterworld, Helen, perfect, virginal, consummate, home, returns this side of living only to stroke her wayward double's hair in the heather, to usher her towards the window in all the houses of ████.

But from her mourning for her lost girlhood companion, Jane is already inoculated to death's disguise by religious fervour: the saviour Helen sends in St. John can only offer a passionless union in service to god's colonial mission.

Over the moors comes Rochester's call of a wild and earthly desire holding its roots in the lands of their ancestors, beckoning her back through the heath. An epilogue leans these genres into one another's shadows.

For Jane, this is a love story. For Helen, it is a tragedy.

iii. On Ghosts

Back again with another dream to bury. You remember what bleeds or bled because you bore it, the gnash in your flesh, the cadaver of south creek, the sternum hollow of the bodies you're teaching yours not to need, the six-foot stars you hammer deeper each time you need to take their bearing. A long way up is a long way down from the burning room, the window from the madman's cage. Something older than our desire reaches with dawning hands through the funeral rooms you've never left, child, child, the light's

co ????????
ming fur
ther awa ———y.

i. Night Cries

What visions plague the mother to cry out in her sleep? Who is coming back for you, Mother?

A withering hand rattles at the plate, a clouded eye glazes over faded photographs.

Jedda is in the room.

Jedda is on the table.

Jedda watched by a perfect, expressionless moon through the flyscreen, forever writing letters to no-one and nowhere, the mail train rattling through the night.

Jedda, all restless sensation, kicking and clanking at the bucket, waving and clasping with her arms, scrubbing and wringing the washing, cackling as she whips the flies and arid earth, gasping as she drags the hose over her hair and skin.

Jedda on the rocks, Jedda wailing in a mess of seaweed and film, sonic panic and the crashing sea, the woman disappeared from the frame, Mother who is coming back for you? Jedda on the platform, Jedda crawled and hunched in her Sunday best as the land breaches and breathes around her. Jedda alone amongst the bones and the dead, the wind howling over watercolour hills.

Jedda is in the room.

Mother, don't you hear her in the room?

ii. Night Cries

Brisbane-born photographer and filmmaker Tracey Moffatt is revered for her work interrogating colonial forms and archival histories of encounter. Her 1990 short film *Night Cries: A Rural Tragedy* is a self-conscious fictionalisation of Charles Chauvel's 1955 film *Jedda*, known in the history of Australian cinema as the first feature film shot in colour, and the first film to star two Aboriginal actors, Rosalie Kunoth-Monks and Robert Tudawali.

Distributed internationally as *Jedda the Uncivilised* and marketed as *the story of Eve in ebony*, Chauvel's film centres on the tragic death of its eponymous protagonist after she is abducted from her white foster family at a cattle station in the Northern Territory by Marbuk, a 'wild' and 'untrustworthy' Aboriginal itinerant labourer. Jedda, a nameless orphan abandoned by a wandering tribe, is handed over to the station's mistress by an Aboriginal domestic worker to salve the grief of her dead white baby. Although raised to repudiate the ways of her people in favour of Aboriginal workers living adjacent to whiteness, as a girl Jedda finds herself unable to repress the call of the bush, or resist the spiritual rites of the tribal world she encounters through Marbuk.

Jedda luxuriates in all the fetishes of the primitive that so intoxicate the Western gaze, affirming a paradigm of Aboriginal masculinity enemy to both white and black worlds: the ultimate spoil of even the most domesticated native belle, unable to overcome her primeval instincts and ultimately falling victim to the destructive telos of Aboriginal savagery.

As Yiman and Bidjara scholar Marcia Langton argues, the film's propaganda lies in its inversion of frontier violence, fixed on Marbuk's repudiation by his own Country and Elders as punishment for pursuing an unsanctioned union. By supplanting Jedda's intended marriage to a half-caste stockman, Marbuk disrupts her assimilation into the sphere of settler society as a reproductive worker. Jedda's death is presented as the senseless but ultimately insurmountable conclusion of a doomed race: a waste of white investment in the civilising mission, a squandering of potential labour for the pastoral frontier. Jedda demonstrates what Jameson calls a master narrative of inevitability, total teleology, whereby colonised subjects are domesticated into the universal horizon of capital growth and production, so as to assimilate the very being of their Indigeneity.

In *Night Cries*, Moffatt stages a speculative reimagining of Jedda's fate, in which our protagonist does not tragically perish at the hands of the noble savage, but survives to care for her elderly white foster mother in the ruins of the pastoral homestead.

In this telling, Jedda spends her days nursing, feeding and toileting the dying woman, taking momentary respite under a tattered flyscreen to read travel magazines and write letters to an unnamed recipient. Moffatt reinverts the social order of Chauvel's frontier through the surreal, referential artifice of the set, in which the pair are watched by Namatjira-esque hills at a kitchen table cluttered with the remnants of cheap canned goods. The cattle, the workers, the rich harvest and capital all gone, the extracted wealth spent. All that remains in the squalor and debris of empire is a hollow frame without signifier, a withering frail once-mistress and the Aboriginal woman who survives her. Somewhere in the distance a train passes by in the night.

Tracey Moffatt's nightmare refocuses our gaze towards the colonial paternalism that underwrites Chauvel's narrative, where Jedda's survival ensures her reproductive service to the matriarch of a decaying pastoral homestead, long after the land has been stripped of its worth. The mother claws the mosquito net and moans through the night. Jedda walks her to and from the outhouse, her movements charged with resentment and overstimulation. Memories press and scrape against her body while Jedda hears dingoes howl beyond the horizon.

As Langton suggests, this telling plays out the anxiety of settlers who removed Aboriginal children from their families and communities for the civilising and assimilationist ambitions of the colony. *Perhaps the worst nightmare of the adoptive parents is to end life with the black adoptive child as the only family, the only one who cares*, she writes. Moffatt, herself an adoptee, projects this nightmare on a stage emblematic of the poverty known intimately to so many Aboriginal people, disrupting fantasies of white benevolence with the materiality of Blak experience.

Plagued by alienation, malaise and traumatic visions that charge the maternal figure with ambivalence, Jedda and the homestead are both tearing at the seams, on the brink of their survival, each haunting the other. When the mother is finally dead, Jedda crawls foetal and sobbing to her side, while around them the Country pulses its heartbeat for the first time.

iii. Night Cries

(x) We are accustomed to the work of excavating shadows from gaps in the louder story.

(x) For many Aboriginal families, our archival presence constellates on two interlinked encounters with the colonial capitalist state: records of our removals from families into reserves, missions, institutions, training schools or prisons, and records of our labour: domestic service, the military, the pastoral properties still drying up the land.

(x) To evidence your existence to the state, you are required to produce archives of what you lost, or what you made.

(x) You are thinking about labour, about death, about desire.

(x) You are always thinking about labour, about death, about desire.

iv. Night Cries

I am not something that fell out of the sky

for the pleasure of somebody putting another culture
into this cultured being.

I am here and now.

Don't try and suppress me, and don't call me a problem.

I am not the problem.

I have never left my country, nor
have I ceded any part of it.

I am not the problem.

(iii) 256GB OF SALVAGED MEMORY

1. An email that finds you grown over by mould.

2. A patch of open sky from the felling of the possum-bearing palm in your neighbour's garden, your dog's fixed gaze on the fenceline as she waits for her old foes to return.

3. The livestream buffering in the church and the mourning wail that still drags you through the floor.

4. The 600m stroll from station to desk automatically indexed by your personal blood-diamond lithium-ion eye. Its grief capture in the text log you cannot delete, the numbers you cannot call.

5. A reparative reading of the AUKUS invoice.

6. A text to your father, 14 October 2023, sent on your way to vote on a constitutionally enshrined mechanism for colonial collaboration: *all I can think of is Palestine.*

7. His answer: *it's a fucked world, but we're standing against the tide.*

8. The tide: 4,500 square kilometres of seabed choked by the rotting carcasses of 15,000 bottlenose dolphins, leafy seadragons, razor clams, surf crabs, hairy mussels and long-finned worm eels.

9. A photoset of cut flowers floating in blue-green waves. Red, pink and orange roses, sunflowers, lilacs, amaryllis. The click through, the test of link rot, the decay of mutuals. At the umbilical stock page, an unfiltered original, cut tags and deleted blood, absent all the abstract aesthetics of disembodied blooms buoyant in a too-blue sea.

10. An image description tangled in a decaying cache that tells you they were scattered in the Mediterranean Sea to honour 106 Syrian and Palestinian refugees who drowned in August 2018 off the Libyan shore. An SEO extract to a deactivated memorial for the 2,337 refugees whose bodies were never recovered that year.

11. *If you are the owner of this domain, please contact your administrator.*

12. The codename index for a spreadsheet charting the doctors and case workers least likely to send in the cops.

13. The cartography of violence that girls map between each other, warnings of dark corners and isolated footpaths, what the disingenuous claim are just *consequence* and *personal responsibility*, what Sharpe calls *acts of care as shared and distributed risk, as mass refusals of the unbearable life, as total rejections of the dead future.*

14. Streetsides lined with rotting bouquets, cards and teddy bears disintegrating in the rain.

15. A groupchat entangled by colleagues and comrades you know only with abstract familiarity, gathering through collective trauma bonds to meet, march, petition and disrupt on repeat.

16. The video we all remember, the first one to strangle your last childish mirage of moral lore: yours, a pair of girls the age of your neighbour's girls, the rest unspeakable without a reckoning, without taking back their land to let them rest again.

17. The rubble of once-was doors and halls and the martyrs rising from the dust.

18. The meta-memories that the machine won't stop highlighting, hyperlinking you back to the bastards, sons of bitches, wreckers, rakes, malingerers and dilettantes you had the misfortune of sharing an image with.

19. The film of ochre dust that coats the facemask you don't wash enough, the clapsticks you strike to call the ancestors to the march, the slow heavy walk of the crowd that shifts your hip back to the bruising angle that wakes you in the night.

20. A reference in your notes app to a video montage you could only bear to watch once, slow sad strings singing sick and heavy in the corner of your belly. Six days and 75 years into the genocide, a library in Gaza writing to their sister library in Barcelona: *we don't know if we'll be able to keep in contact from now on, so please tell the following generations about us.*

21. The dead link to the memory, the ghost record in the predictive AI you can't turn off.

22. The wedding gift of Venice drowned beneath the weight of ninety-six private jets.

23. Your call log to 13YARN and every variation of *you need to go home* you've refused to hear.

24. The flinch of your belly synapses when you meet a █████ who moves like him. All day dragging your pattern-seeking body through the tracks of it, blind but not deaf in the dark.

25. Scenes on repeat in the crumbling walls of your mind, leaking their cadences into your mouth:

    a. An unnamed worker in a chef's coat on the streets of LA, facing off to a line of FBI and ICE agents abducting all those who look like them, *I'm sure your mama starved in the past. That's why she came here,* anger and despair moving through him as he strikes his own face and the cops reassure each other. *I can see the fucking shame in your fucked-up face, puto. I see the shame in you. But tell your mama how you're proud of corralling people.*

    b. Leigh Evans, a nurse, weeping and begging before a line of guards at the Rafah border, *the women are trying to feed their dying babies and their breasts are empty, do you know what that smells like,* the camera zooming in on the shamed faces of the Egyptian forces and the cries of those assembled from the Global March for Gaza: *for humanity and for love, stand for your brothers and sisters in Falasteen.*

c. Hadeeqa Arzoo Malik leading the chants against a wall of New York cops outside CUNY, *we read the badges of the pigs, so to the Rahmans and the Muhammads, to the Alis and the Abdullahs, to the Rafids, to the Rafids, to the pigs,* and one cop steps forward to relieve his colleague Rafid from the line, as if a cop can ever know solidarity, can ever be forgiven for the humanity they forgot was theirs also to bear, as if there is a corner of the earth small enough for a cop to hide their shame.

26. The blank space on your tongue for the eulogies you can't stop writing, the jagged teeth of history up in your guts, your frail foolish gestures to keep your grief somewhere it will not bruise the world.

27. Nour Salman on the library steps, *the earth has betrayed us, Palestine is a people bidding themselves goodbye,* and beyond the manufactured skyline of the city, the clouds assembling. Your hands, folding and refolding your niece's keffiyeh over her shoulders, never settled or satisfied by the fit, just fussing and moving so she doesn't see your stricken face, so you can give your hands something still living to cling to.

28. The revolutionary letter pinned behind your desk so you never pass a workday without the reminder that *empire is its own undoing.*

before

You turn to me, my gaze meets your gaze.
You are in the doorway. I am in the room. You come to me.
This is an old story.

after

I turn to you, your gaze meets my gaze.
I am in the doorway. You are in the room. I come to you.
This is an old story.

Ache

Every story gets smaller when you lose those you tell it for. Since we were here last, I've buried almost every cardinal point. I told you I was speaking between deaths.

I come to you now from the shadow that stretches across the campfires in the sky to ask: do I have you? Like you I have been made to swallow the grief and product of the world from a screen.

As you did I woke in a world that watches without mercy. As you will I learnt who did the withholding, who profits from your pain.

Like you I have seen the limit of our reach, the frailty of wrist.

Like you I have bought and sold and traded for a peace that was never intended for us to hold.

Like you I have sought to summon back an embrace made for me by mothers, an archive like a womb.

We are not, perhaps, in every way, *we*. I welcome your exhaustion, your suspicion, your throat, your gaze.
They also want this, your attention.

Do I have you? Are you with me? Do you understand,
this is yours to carry as well?

iii. hip

I wake forgetting where and when I am, my throat scratched with screams from the 3am panic the visions shuttering between scenes of carnage crushing against the bodies of those I love most and a replay of every failed social gesture, the paralysis of every delayed task collapsing into the next, emails full of asks or kindnesses I've left to ferment that sickly hardened lock in my jaw I grind through the night, all fray and jet fuel, already late for whatever I agreed to, the hotel sleek and insufferable and air-conditioned, the debris of public personas still scattered through the room, I am standing heaving grasping at the doorway and yet I am still somehow always also in the bush across from the old house again, those flames licking up the bearded dragon tree, still burning I assemble against a soundtrack that's been circling in my brain for weeks – *it's how we have to live versus living with ourselves* – again, again, nothing resolved or incorporated I am crawling from the latest in an assortment of foreign beds that fuck up my hip, I am raw exposed flesh not a body but an ever-tightening bow waiting to release in full, violent force I am opening closing wounds I am so much smaller than I will let myself be I—

Analysis Act One

(i) There are things I refuse to give language but still sit stubborn adamantine in their place of becoming. Everything I commit to the page is grasping at the spectre of our orality. Everything I gulp from the air is always already inscribed.

(ii) This is a long wound of mine. I always cry when I'm given the mic.

(iii) Who would I tell it to? The brushtails, the chrysalis, the smudge of ash on your brow? I'd rather have a night I can fold into, a mouthful of violets, a gun for that second screen.

(iv) Take back those words I won't need where I'm going. Compromise, tolerance, the vocabulary of awareness raising, concession, reprieve. All that endless striking against the purity thresholds of the radical and revolutionary, my stumbling through autopsies and shards of mirror, the ache in my wrist from all that refreshing of the page.

(v) It was never going to end a different way. We ate the hard and fibrous fruit because we wanted some kind of flesh so fucking bad.

(vi) If there are words for this they're not mine. I can't find it in my throat, but I feel it in my teeth when Hindi writes *I know I'm American because when I walk into a room something dies.* I keep backing away from the colony and pulling at my flesh to get it out. In my sleep I was told that I paid for the bombs. When I woke there was no nightmare.

(vii) Where can you go without their gaze? What do you have left that is yours to keep?

(viii) I'll tell you what I've finally learnt, what I'd been told all along. It will take an action so wide the centre will not hold.

(ix) A river never forgets where it runs.

Analysis Act Two

The colony tells us everything that can be dug up must be made useful – oil, metal, pain. *Everything points back to pain*, says that essay I keep holding reluctant in my jaw.

I only went back to therapy because J couldn't handle my lack of progress on the second round of medication, the blue-black weight that never shifted out the door, the voices in the invisible other room after three nocturnal months.

The second psych's office was in the community hall where I took painting classes as a child. There was still a bruise on the floor where I'd knocked over a shelf fourteen years ago. I picked him from a list read aloud by the rotational GP at the medical centre because his name sounded Aboriginal. He wasn't, and they never are, but he was nice, and he asked me to talk about my family, and if he hadn't told me to be gentle on myself I could have stayed. Later I discovered he'd worked with my mother for years, that he'd treated my sister.

It's not betrayal but it's context, like when the first psych responded to my anxiety, intergenerational trauma, disordered eating and undiagnosed autoimmune condition by giving me a quiz for empaths, like how they now sell essential oils over facebook.

The story about the oil-selling psychologist is a favourite for the right crowd, like that Christmas at Nan's with the sawn-off shotgun, or chasing J down the night he disappeared in a manic episode to take cocaine with a former child soldier. I keep anecdotes in my back pocket for parties and the staff break room. Sometimes the performance arrives before I've incorporated all the wounds I only remember in the telling. I don't think in language so this is how I process, how I fold back the damage into my menu of personalities and assure whoever I meet that I'm nothing to be worried about – a little strange, a little raw, but my selectively overexposed life should be neither envied nor pitied. I am a light that turns on and off by sensor, a dog baring teeth in her sleep. I keep forgetting the rooms I'm in. At night the meta-reading of every encounter is restaged in vaudeville – I dream in movements and violence but the scream never arrives, I didn't make it to the bridge this time.

Jamison writes that *my wounds are fertile*. This annoys me, is exhausting in its indulgence, the West's extraction fetish. And yet I keep daring myself to write the things I don't want to say, those memories with place and teeth that keep announcing themselves in my sleep. I tried it that day I read the review claiming I'd made myself unknowable, never interrogating the critique, just pressing forward at the first available desire path to grip unsteady to a podium twenty minutes into a seven-minute slot explaining the asbestos curse to a room of strangers, unable to find the trace of the story back to the mouse in my kitchen, knowing I should never have tried to hold so much blood in my trembling hands.

I gave up therapy so this is my tense to shift. To renew the tired threads I keep trying to weave a home from. I don't have a good gauge on trauma etiquette or my tolerance for beer. I have to remind myself to ask appropriate questions, I'm reluctant to trust █████, I can't stop obliging people I hate. I never abandoned the semiotics of malnourishment – *taking recourse in bone-as-language* – I never softened my ritual of paranoia – *we can't stop imagining new ways to hurt.*

Call it pessimism of the intellect and optimism of the dumb bitch because I wasted so much time trying to leave my memories in the ground, thinking they wouldn't find their way back. None of them are mine anymore: when the poem is gobbled into the machine it will spit back statistical probabilities from my subtext, will show the reader where to find the bodies.

Baldwin said you must learn *to write a sentence as clean as a bone.* He didn't know what would be coming to feast, the algorithm trained on that grand unified theory of female pain – *girl gets; girl gets; girl gets.* The holy prayer of women, colonisers and collaborators alike.

Jamison: *This hurts; I hate saying that.* And fuck it. It isn't easy to be Blak and believed, to say *there is violence here, on this street, in this text, in the structure of this world.* I can admit this was a wound I didn't deserve, but I still don't feel I've earnt this pain. The window to speak it was so fragile, the water murky from all that malaise. We are always trafficking in the fetish before the commodity, washing our hands in new blood. Nothing so beautiful as a threshold and compartmentalised desire, all traumas and transcendence in the dying machine. It's rich feed alright, a bumper sticker and a tote for every sad girl in the world.

I looked up from grief and shame to discover myself already marked by another empire in mirage. At least I get to choose the brand of the bullet, the avatar for my carbon debt.

It's what rots in the wound – the limit, the cautious habit to fold back: I want to want a long future for myself, but I've been taught to settle for a living I won't need to grieve.

Analysis Act Three

(i) Prynne: *no poet has or can have clean hands, because clean hands are themselves a fundamental contradiction. Clean hands do no worthwhile work.*

(ii) In the crisis of social, ethical and ecological collapse that greets us daily, clean hands suggest a mode of simplicity that sinks against its own cost.

(iii) The machine keeps trying to hide things from you. Your memories, your knowing, your humanness.

(iv) Statistical certainty says that by the time this book is published, ancient forests will have burnt to dust, more Blakfullas will be executed by the state, another dead girl in a creek, another billion sent off in our names to help Israel turn Gaza into a memory. Don't mistake this for anything less than sanctioned violence, for anything more than the state functioning as was always intended.

(v) Every night I type the text I never send, begging my parents to tell me how to live with this, to tell me how to survive a world that arrived uninvited, that took up laws so that we might not speak, that took up arms so we might not stand, that took up air so that we might not breathe.

(vi) I keep meeting you here. In this fatality of distance, in the cruelty of a restful night.

(vii) Sutherland: *that it has come to this is your fault, you who know how to read this.*

(viii) Every day I ask myself what the machine doesn't want me to know. Every tomorrow will be the day I find a way to learn it. Every night I read poetry just to give my hands something to do.

(ix) Refusal, resistance, disavowal and survivance are tenors of a liveable life. In action they are compromised, bloody-handed, in the world and of it.

(x) These are not metaphors, these are demands, they are the furies that keep me from sleep, that take my hand in the dark and guide me first through grief, then to work.

WHAT YOU CAN DO WITH YOUR HANDS

1. First, verify. Count the fingers, the sharpness of the lines, check for smudges or extra limbs. Is there a blur? A hollow aura where the wrong light strikes? What shadows loom from an open door? Wear eucalyptus on your wrist, invoke that old verse. Don't swallow the fruit. Don't make deals with their kind.

2. Temple, brows, slide index fingers down the nasal canal, swipe thumbs under the eye. Push harder than you think you should. Swallow. It will hurt until it won't.

3. Take every opportunity to build your callus. When you pass through somewhere you're not already known, press your palm against the bark, mark your skin. Say hello, say you are grateful for the care.

4. Learn to repair. Darn, patch, dart, stitch. What you own has a story that begins before you – flax, oil, timber, sand – molecules assembling and rearranging long before market demands. How many winters will this keep you warm? How many generations will it take to decay? Keep that history on your back as long as you can, the growth of the earth, the craft of workers, the smell of lovers. Learn to read the inner and outer sides of weaving. Something in your fingers can remember the way we used to care for what we needed, will explain the motion for you.

5. Flour and water if it's all you've got. Butter, salt, milk or beer, if you can get it. Press in with your palm, fold back with fingers, keep your touch light. Let it rest a while. Place the oven at the edge of the coals. Eat with what you have, share with who you can.

6. You will be asked if you want to throw soil into the grave. The first time you will decline, choosing instead to watch the magpies prune the dust, afternoon heat rising through the trees. When you're here again the dirt will sit under your fingernails for weeks while the flowers rot in the kitchen.

7. Always learn how to unfold the window latch before you need to climb through it in the dark.

8. If you keep a knife, know it might be used against you, as evidence, as weapon. Refuse parables of tolerance and hold with a straight wrist. Don't draw before you need it again. Watch the other limbs. Understand but do not rely on the geography of the blade, concentrations of shale, movements of copper.

9. Every day check for soreness or changes in the breast tissue. Every day repeat the motion of bending your hips back in their swollen joints.

10. Secure the scene, try to disinfect your hands. If the wound is yours, imagine it isn't. Place the panic somewhere safe to return to. If it's theirs, steel your stomach, turn your head to breathe, look. Don't underestimate the skull, don't overestimate the spine. Is the skin torn wide like a collapsing state or just scraped with ordinary chaos? Let it bleed for a breath or two. Clean it well: rinse with water or saline if your gods or comrades came prepared. Soap gentle around the wound. Pluck out dirt, rubble, glass, the small violences. Think of it as meat if you must, tender sinews, proof of impact. Antiseptic reeks of empire, hydrogen peroxide hisses like a tiger snake startled on the path, iodine and alcohol sting like a bitch, but so does being alive. Use whatever you can get: this is survival, not purity. Wrap in what is clean, change daily. Watch for heat, redness, swelling, the body's omens. Heed it all and treat what you can. Befriend medics, witches, mothers. If you can't manage it, assist those who will, gather up the bruised instead, take down the names of children. Keep the rot away from healing wounds.

11. Soak the wick in kerosene, use storm-proof matches and a ballast weight. Petrol can be diluted with detergent or nail polish remover. The burl is the strongest bone of a tree, the best barrel for a bat.

12. Pick up your fucking litter.

13. Approach gently. Meet their eyes, softly murmur the kindest things you store under your bed. Allow yourself to become familiar. Body-double the growth patterns of moss, the melting of snowflakes, the unfurling of a rare bloom. If you must move, be a silk nightgown swaying in an evening breeze, nuclear radiant in the moonlight. Offer blessings of seed and fruit. Become patient, sturdy. Say, 'I won't let the world abandon you again.' Say, 'I will take your loneliness, I have so much time for you in my life.' Let the tenderness of the earth hum within you, remember how you once were cradled. Be confident, take hold from above, encasing their wings and cupping the breast. If your pigeon is injured, tell the vet you want to save them, that you value their lives and won't forget all the labour they were conditioned to perform. Tell them, don't you know that pigeons dream? Explain the hollow you have waiting, all the sticks and hair and soft things you lined it with. They dream of flying, of coming home.

14. Remove your grip from your own throat.

15. Hold mine. Wait with me just a little while. I need to tell you about a door.

Ark

(x) Arise and avenge new archons of the archive striding the stony rubbish of the once-was archontic authority. Look how strong you've made your hands, how much your arms can bear.

(x) In your life you will be called into relation with those who would seek to degrade you, by those who would make themselves the world.

(x) Between us is a *we* who trembles, and one of us is afraid of the dark.

(x) Call this into being: my resentment, your reluctance, your always searching eye and the place in the soil where you can put this down. My love, I could not blame you for your loneliness, for the way you raised your chin when their hands were at your throat.

(x) Who could blame you for your rage? Who more than girls know what is withheld from the final story? There are oceans more blood than they wrote beloved, more than those masters could make footnote from girls in perfect radiate hieroglyphics, each hour of the clock a woman's tooth claimed by fatal blush, more than those techno-fascist space lords launching rockets against island girls standing steadfast as seawalls in the rising shore, more than their holy blessed primal fathers gnashing teeth at the stolen girls still cowered in the church.

(x) Girls, we need you to be useful: there is so much to assemble, so much we must take back.

(x) My love, my love, I do not blame you but, my love, I cannot let you rest.

UNFOLDINGS

Those Who Will Die After

you who surface from rubble of rubble
digital echoes of genesis told
third hand to lyrebirds
scratching water from clay
i pass my time this side of living
waiting for a way to be home eternal
to lay in the roots of that old gum
& guard you as best i can
through the old nights hurtling
their debris & dust in your eyes

        i admit there's no
        way to make it soft

tell future ghosts the sun gave us
what it said it would the sea wanted
what we knew it did
    the statistical certainty
    the dawn sold for oil
i'll say i am sorry we let us drink at
holograms i'm sorry we let them code god

the bullets the bombs the drones the
tanks the planes the gas the boots boots boots your finite
inheritance our looming spectres firework red mist on the
cave wall

there is still so much honour here
    & i have seen resistance in
    the earth dusting from my
    sister's dancing feet

i am afraid but
i have had so much time
to despair you to hum your name to the ash
to keep what i can from the cops

    so much time to stitch myself to you
    through the dark this is planting
    seed & song

                this is refusing
    to leave

as you must refuse
to leave

Antidotes for Despair

i.

I call and you answer, my marrow raw
and stupid and heavier than the world,
my parts disintegrating into the ether,
it is never my fault I always say, but
some days it will be my fault, that's
the law of nature, the deal we made,
someone had to suffer for something
righteous and someone else will ride
up for the feast. I call and you answer
and I try to shape the fragmenting
waves, say I am trying so hard, say I
have only done what I could, and you
will say *yes*, and you will say *I know*,
and you will say *so what do we need
to do next*, despite my wails and all
the nothing I say to have left, the seas
that rise and the nights lit up from the
blasts, the griefs ripping up the carpet
and hounding at the door, the mould
that grows in my teeth and all the fires
of the earth now thrashing in my gaze,
all the pity I can summon all the rage
I can hold, and you will wait and again
you will say *yes*, and *I know*, you let me
howl because there is nothing else but
what do we need to do next.

ii.

Every day gets easier. The muscle strains, this time you answer the phone. You can stay a little longer if you want, there's more tea in the pot. You always forget how that first breeze arrives, what it takes on its way. This week you should consider the moon, the light and rhythms it sings to the sea. You keep trying to explain the hunger but can't stop describing a door. There's much to do with yearning, the emancipation of your life, for September sun to bathe our calves and for a gentle night we can keep from the cops. There are many ways to name love, even more to consume. Stay a while, this waiting is safe here. I want to hear about your door.

iii.

I'll tell you this one for nothing but the pale reddish hope steaming from the hills, blurring roos still soaring in their dreams. These trees have seen things you and I can't believe. Sky unfolds for gang-gangs taking their course, the water past our sight rolling as it will always know how. It will always soon be night, more dawn will light the dew. A record isn't always a home, sometimes it's shadows and nights of memory fading into the creek, the blossom of gum humming its sweetness into the breeze. It might be all we have. Isn't that so very much?

iv.

Ink, amethyst, haze on the mountain spine, yellow butter and bread. Afternoon dangled veranda and your mouth, that golden wine. Bare feet on sandstone shelf, her name the old way, lomandra scraping calves. Last year's burn rusts up the bark while Joan sings Bobby from the shed. Tea-tree in your hair. We eat tomatoes with fat lumpy pasta rolled by palm, jirrajirra preens the grass. Blotted eucalypt, semolina on my wrist. Your mouth, my mouth, everything we survived for this.

Losing Dogs

my baby my baby you're my baby
say it to me
I say to the humid bath air
to the dog asleep under the moon
          seaweed rose jam white claws
          and you, mitski
in your amber halo of misery
the prophet of rotting girls

last night I promised I would not drink tonight
weep in the bath eat dinner or scroll the void
I want to feel it,
          I tell the tiles and the mould
as if there's choice but to keep
bracing against the world
the algorithm we taught what we could bear

I bet on losing dogs
you croon slow and sad
so let's raise a glass to that
to these the oldest themes and the worst

but for that light, the moon, the dogs
the groupchat where we account our days
a redbelly stretching the fire trail
my nephew kicking his first ball
in another screen a boy the same age
his land his history his limbs   torn apart on livestream

mitski, this was always meant to be unliveable
this was never going to hold our gaze back

oh my baby my baby
it's hard to bathe with a body full
of body horror
but maybe somewhere there is a
room unclouded by grief
by girls disintegrating into banality

mitski, how much of this world was
meant to be ours at all?
on my way back from the rally
I am told your father was in the CIA
I want this to be apocryphal
but today I marched for Gaza
while mourning a vote I didn't want
a history I'll never accept
and you are so far away in America
the imperial killing machine

it is unforgiveable to be so weak
to float my body in grief
for living loving mothers
sinking the agony indulgence   while
you echo across cracked tiles
while I am not thinking of the horror
by thinking of rivers   thinking
of kissing your tears forever
thinking   if we can survive our minds
then we should just drown together
so clean at last so fresh my baby
my baby   my baby

my buoyant rage
my blunt witnessing of history
          mitski, give me the power to avenge
          these things I cannot live with

if you gave me back those howling hours
I would howl again

One day the books will count the dead

but not the killers,
will pass over the
weapons,
the death mongers,
the megatons of
carbon and fire
and steel, will
sing sorry songs
for crimes they denied
were ever
certain, won't name
names but show you
faces in black
and white and
never colour,
never blood or
rage. The books
of the forgetful
future will mourn
lost stories,
burning libraries,

shattered schoolrooms,
olive trees
where once the slaughtered
nestled in the roots
to listen to the wind,
will take
pains to mourn every
child taken
while curled in beds
and arms
where once they
read stories written to
remember, to grow
the seeds that nourish
the scorched soil.
If we let them, the
books will grieve what
they'll say was inevitable,
unstoppable, unfathomable,
but they won't tell
the fury and the fight,
what those children
begged the world to
witness. If we let
them they'll ask how
we could have
let it happen.
If we let them
they will do it again,
and will ask us again,
however did we let them.

I'm summoning Sofia Tolstoy from the bath with a spell I bought off Etsy

is how I would say I'm not coping
again if we still needed language to translate
words for void. The glossary of decay I've been soft
launching on the gram still stumbles at the
earnest, lest my grief triggers another sponsored
post for bedazzled pill dispensers and I really
do it this time. The algorithm knows all women
are born to girlmoss on a windy heath but
prefers us labouring forms and substacks
on just enough dexamphetamines to restrain
our violence in the classics aisle.
We are all prisoners to longings that outstretch
the living world, of horrors we traded for desire.
How much of our humanness do we lose

by begging for its memory? The gaps in the
archive for the months and years you were
too tired to write, your hand sore from
his drafts, your breasts cracked and bleeding
from his sons. For all my misery I never had
to write someone else's revolution from the
nursery. Those irresistible laws of strangeness
and fray, sending ████ to the woods and
girls further into themselves. It took me so long
to love my comrades of the flailing frontal-lobe
coalition, sexy babies bare of blood or hair, quiet
mothers or dead Madonnas in the creek. *One cannot*
live by love alone, says a woman left alone in her love.
Sofia, did you ever get to write a line you knew you could
keep for yourself? Everyone has a story we're waiting
for death to tell, for the chance to paint the walls,
to make a girlhood safe and thrilling at last. *Patience*,
you tell yourself, *we were at least blessed with a happy past.*
Did he imagine you on the tracks when
he raged, the light shuttering as the train
roars above you? *I eat once a day, I go nowhere.*
I could bewitch you from history and leave a gap so
wide some ████ would never know their own
minds. Your agonies of spirit folded in with his
shirts. We are all fermenting a mother's rage
and hers before, soaking half-moons on the
palm. You gave your life in double and still
he banished you from the dying room.
Who amongst us hasn't prayed to be destroyed by
a dark we cast ourselves? Sofia, I hope you
left the last pages empty. I hope you never
gave them another word.

Change Agent

Be prepared
to be the worst person
at every party.
Forget the rule of threes,
your clavicle in soft light,
where you left the lighter.
You've been unravelling
since the steam engine,
the coming of those tall ships.
There's no time
for complacency in the
age of rotting stars.
You are already unbearable,
ironising New Year's ins
and outs, your fluency
in microtrends.
Is my body the smallest it could be?
Who wants to fucking know!
There is profit in keeping you weak,
in product placement at the sit-in.
Everything's a recession indicator
to a recession machine.
The revolution needs more than
the hypervigilance of the hottest
orb in the fruit market.
It's so serious to be alive,
so brittle and imperative.
Every day we are paid
to betray each other,

every day someone will try to
leave you in the cold.
You must educate yourself
on surge-level management
and the mangroves,
the blasting of Juukan Gorge.
Be ungovernable and
aligned with orcas. The work is
relational and forever. Some enemies
can be made comrades, or at least
a coalition against the same boot.
Some just want to wear the boot.
There was no rental of the earth,
there is profit in starvation and fear,
in feeding Rowling's black mould.
It bears repeating what labour
you've been made to exchange
for it all, the toll this had
on your hands. I am sorry there
will be more still to do.
Every day resist normalisation
and let yourself be rescued
by the frailest of hopes.
If you're reading this, it's too late,
we cannot forgive your malaise.
If you think you can outlive
this, if you know a cavern somewhere
or have buried some gold in the hills,
I hope this poem claws you every
night. How far could you carry
the heaviest thing you love?
Is that going to be far enough?

Jinda

Aunty outside the church tells me
she held my sister's hand while
she wept when the plane crossed Bundjalung
the gum tree of her story is as holy
as the other holies

I know her the way this cold city makes
me dress strange, demands things from a body
that knows it's not where it's from

                                        most things are
adjacent to rivers – the reflection of root and branch,
the failure of nation, our stuttered inflections as we
practise the old words our grandfather was never taught

my sister's sister tells her the names of lakes
that are healing, has a photo of us at NAIDOC two
decades ago, squinting into winter sun. Driving to
the scar trees my phone lights up with their
names, teasing each other for pulled faces and crude
cut fringes. A year of lonely and I have filled
every corner of the house with mattresses

when I take that flight
I study the pattern of rivers for spines
the window a triangle of memory
map and wordbook:

(stars/stars/stars)
balun yuna-hla ggihl-a dugan-dah
the river [milky way] runs
between the mountains
(stars/stars/stars)

my sister taught my dog to swim in the river
her namesake kneads into the valley I know like
our own hands

most things are adjacent—
some woven together, like the basket she made
that sits by my bed in the cold city. I know nothing
more holy. I have my father's feet
and my mother's mouth.

Aunty said she would have known me
anywhere by my sister's eyes.

I Won't Use These Drafts for Your Eulogy

O my love, you keep saying so low and soft,
just to hear how it sounds in a room. Every night
a moon, somewhere an ambulance, somewhere
a cockatoo folding into its sleep. Every night a
big hard thorny cross to drag while our
dog smuggles stones into the bed.

I keep rewriting the poem. My anxiety, your
rapid-cycling-polar-axis, the years we'll spend
watching the fires, the children we couldn't bear
teaching to survive. You keep saying this
is a good run on the life you'd parlayed,
tallying years against headstones, your mangle
of griefs. A third of mine has been spent holding
you, the old nights making you in my dreams.

O my love, this one is still heavy on my tongue,
the mercy–love relation, the mourning work
I keep trying to hoard from the dawn. Even in
exile I'm never not listening to you finding
every pothole in the sea. Somewhere in the
aftermath of language you found a way
to tell me there is no peace in the world.
Somewhere in the dark you reach for me,
so low, so soft, and you are mine.

R400

Sleek stabled axis of perfect mortality your nimble lethalities outstrip market competition // terminus of occidental alchemy / the prehistory of an abstract death sings each sum to two-kilometre-limit access // supple / seraphic / Icarian at barely four hundred kilograms // light enough to evangelise the tectonic firepower of the thirty-millimetre / the 7.62mm coaxial machine // come gather soldiers your grenades will be automatically launched / your anti-tank missiles guided // surface-to-air communicable effectors plug and play to our wide range of electro-optic accessories / four-axis-stabilised-lock-turret level to uncompromised lethality sub-milliradian accuracy // this baby could kill a baby from a mile away / pictured here powdered crème brûlée fresh from the box // buy and trade your piece of AUKUS empire riches of kings / a share in the final term of sanguine equation aeons in the drafting // you must pity us, for what we

Instructions on Getting a Gun

You're right we weren't built for this
but muscle is a thing that hurts to grow.
How you gonna kill the cop in

your head if you won't sleep long
enough to see the whites of her eyes?
We're all tired of baking bread,

shedding the liberal consensus of
poetic form, harvesting scraps of verse
from calorie logs. The worst minds

of our generation are cops or
real estate agents, want us
to delay resistance until the

readings are done. If you
own a weapon you must learn to
use it with ease and skill, without

hesitation. We have so much skin to
shed, so many antidotes to
despair. Stop telling them what you'd

give to be beautiful, demand what you
need to live. Don't say girlboss, say fuck
the police. Say glory, say holy, say

I know this is not my grief alone.
If you don't own a weapon make friends.
If you don't have friends consider how you

have made enemies, learn how
to offer aid. This is all a function of
an intended purpose, the machine operating

to its own design. Understand it will take
everything, forbearance, humility, acts of
shared and distributed risk, losing what

you thought you needed to survive. It won't
feel like it, but one day you'll discover you
can miss something without needing it back.

Repeat it every night. We will never survive
this without each other. What will there be to
survive without each other?

Uplock Actuator System

We aren't sending weapons, they said,
just the only lock for the only door that
opens when they are fired from the air.

In footage the sky in Palestine is blue
and forever. I want to think of Palestine
as olive trees and mallow on the hills.

Like you I have watched the limit of the world
from a screen. When you woke there was no
limit, no laws for the intimate machines of empire,

for the carnage debted to our days. Like you I have
fought not to lose myself to complacency, to settle
the worried well. As you did so I calculated

the cost, the carbon and the lead, the percentage of
my wage, the parts in the bag. In Palestine the
blue sky roars like a dying star. In a parallel

occupation the worker labours for and with machines
to strip blood from the land. One portion for the mines,
one for weapons, two for the privilege of a drought

and who fucking knows for submarines. Yesterday the
gunjis shot another black man in the street, designated areas
to stop and detain. Every colony is built of wire and

bolted doors. My country is full of blue sky and shrapnel,
ingredients for bombs. A housing crisis on stolen
land. Every colony is a sky full of fire and restless

martyred spirits. Empire slaughters generations while
colonisers send your wages to the machine. This
deserves no forgiveness, is a force to be resisted.

Don't let them say this was only a piece.

Glory Be The Girlypop

this one's for the girlypops of the fifteen-minute cities and
the future we know will outlive us //

the date-night girlypops
watching genocide and revolution back to back

(thinking constantly of dying)

holding the wineglass to amber light //

the maladaptive daydream girlypops
drowning in a green-tile plunge pool

cooking pasta in frank lloyd wright's kitchen the girlypops
of forgotten gods and ladders the wife of the reaper the
sower of bells //

now this is something i can air-fry
the girlypop says to the
moon //

in the dream we have forgiven our mothers
(in the nightmare we are become her)
destroyer of worlds and blood heavy with lead //

the crimes of what was done to her to make us like this
the kind of living that cuts the mouth

// there's no horizon for the girlypops where we wake at
dawn and know we will not have to leave again / no place to
care for and protect //

it's a comfortable life for the girlypops
(according to the movement of capital)

but most days we want to go home to a home that is
disappearing   that is all windows and doors
closed to the world //

in the fifteen-minute city all the girlypops read the poem
ungenerously   we do not own the windows we close
we know the dark times will be for screaming

// hold hands when we weep at the riot
compare our ferritin levels in bars //

each of us has known a kind of violence //

we are not forgiving our mothers
we are grieving them along with the world

/ the movement of capital the lead the moon   the things
we wish poetry could do for violence

// poetry as a domestication of affect
// poetry as an anagram of someone else's pain
// poetry as a promise to remember the version we prefer
// lying as a way of living with ourselves
    poetry as a way of living with each other
    through years that will be structured by extinction
    by hardened lumps of microplastics collecting in
    our graves //

it is quiet and frail to say we didn't want this
    we wanted to be beautiful we wanted to be safe //

we the girlypops are lucky

        we will get less time than we want

        (but there will still be time)

// i will love you as hard as i can

        my girlypops my mother the moon

        //

                //

//

//

// glory be to girlypops gaslighting

too close to the sun /

// glory be to daughters of mothers who struck
back /

/ who knew the cost of being girls

givers of the grief inheritance //

// glory be to what you have survived

glory be to those who did not //

I Will Love

After June Jordan

when the last flag falls
   it will be death
   or love

      you will no more endure the well-intentioned
      nor wait for tears to dry

pray the nightmare is eloquent from
their lunar-module ships counting windmills of ghostfunds
all
   the crushed nests of sealungs in their eyes

         you have examined your fibres to
         know you are holy of love

you will not placate the complacent nor
withhold your stumbled fragile rage

you are not made to break bread with motherfuckers
but to make yourself the threat of love

this life bade you confess crimes of rulers
like a peppered moth evolving its dust
while you stood a smothered candle in the burning church
mouthing the answerless demands you were asked to ask
each side of a closing door

here now in the tailwind of the trespass
decide it will be love

have no fear for the limit of your grasp
no worry for the breach of mercy or
shame to dilute desire
have love

when there's no-one to absolve
they will say they loved them all
every sorry angel each hallowed
shroud the carnage scrubbed clean from the
square

in your survival you are rinsing grief
until the water runs clear   ordaining the pyre
for a desert burnt in your name

it will be easy to concede to
incentivised collapse   but perhaps

you will bite the glass   kick up your feet

spit in their eye   and love

hair long or none   and only roses with thorns
be loved like salt   a thirst in the dry
a keen in the bite a tongue a cheek   a love   loved as if
                    it were not weak to take yours in
love
to let it claw you back in the dark

            you will tire and hunger and love
            you will grow old   skin to thin and
            bones to crack
            whatever beauty you learnt
before you could refuse   will be borne back
you will keep lights you made for yourself

grow seed in the ash
from this rot grow love

suffer a million little tragedies
            hold the nail of
a million little griefs   you will love each one with
more room for more love

                        swear it
                        commit this to your
                    flesh

        until love kills you you will love

until love kills you you will love

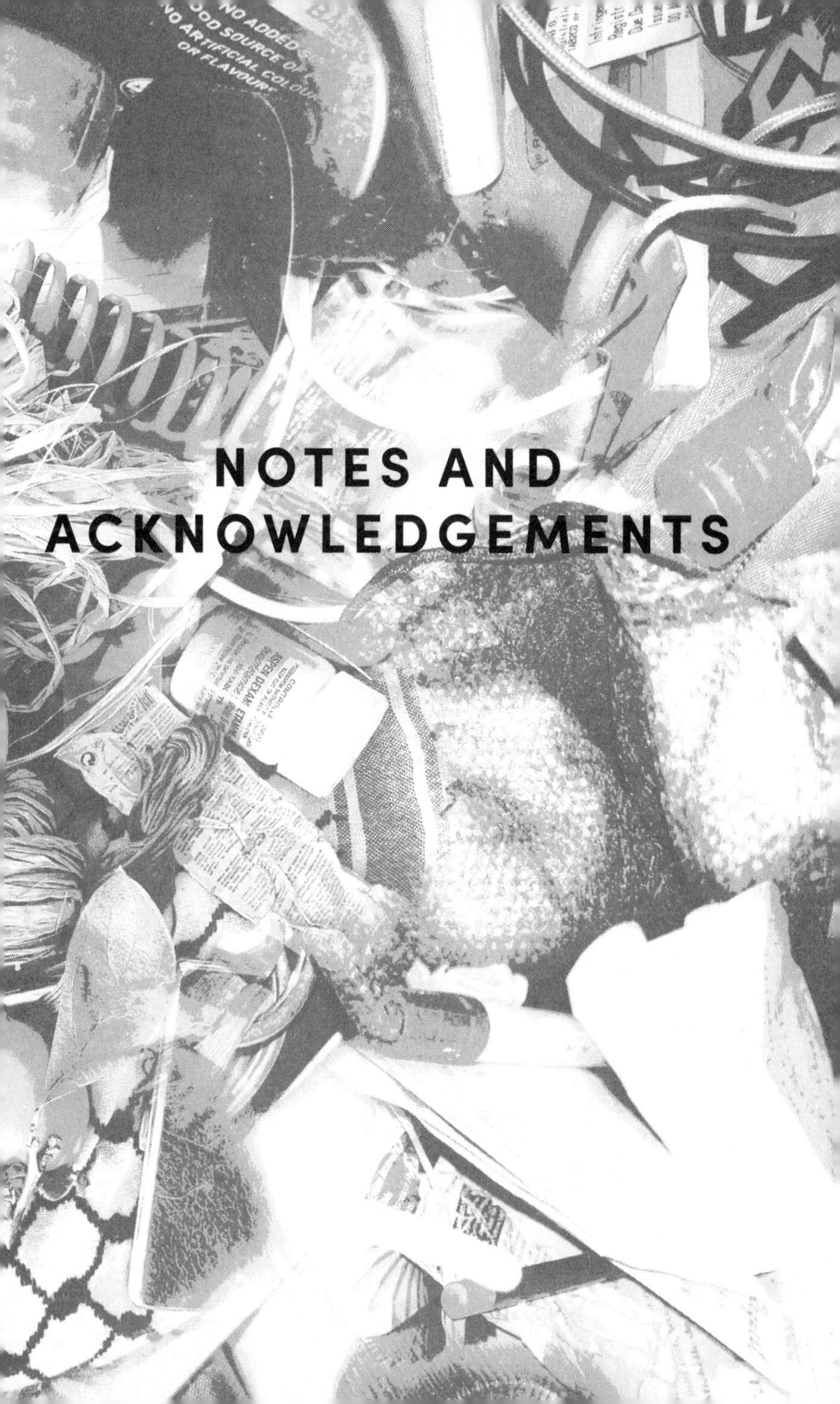

NOTES AND ACKNOWLEDGEMENTS

Disclaimer

No grant or agency paid for this work. I wrote it predominantly on the lands of the Wurundjeri, Woi Wurrung and Boonwurrung peoples of the Kulin Nation. I wrote it on annual leave, I wrote it at home and on Country, I wrote it on a desk that I found on the side of the road, on my phone in the bath. By purchasing or borrowing this book, know that you'll be sending money to families in Gaza, you'll be helping me travel home for funerals, buy treats for my nieces, and save up to buy land where I can grow things and make a safe place for the possums.

Disclaimer

Notes on Citations

Almost all poems in this collection were composed following 7 October 2023, and contain references to events, videos and images that have subsequently disappeared or have proven impossible to source due to technocratic censorship and the interference of artificial intelligence-powered search engines. But we'll never forget what we've seen. I affirm my deepest reverence for the labour and sacrifice of Palestinian journalists recording the horrific crimes of Israel's genocidal regime in Gaza and the West Bank. Every word was written in the attempt to witness Palestinian resistance and survival against the crushing brutality of empire. I commit my life to honouring their spirits and to the liberation of Palestine.

The poems and fragments of this collection were composed in response to a critical mass of literary and digital media works I consumed with unhealthy intensity following the publication of my previous collection. The following is a list of books, essays, authors, videos and discographies that were central to my process of developing this collection. Some of these works I read uneasily, some I inspected and swallowed with such greed I think they're now a part of my DNA. I am collating these citations to acknowledge their strange and rich influences, which have manifested both directly and indirectly in this work:

Kaveh Akbar, various poems

Evelyn Araluen, my old tumblr account as well as various digital archives

James Baldwin, *Notes of a Native Son*, *The Fire Next Time*, various interviews

Hera Lindsay Bird, *Hera Lindsay Bird*
Sean Bonney, everything, but especially *Our Death* and *Letters Against the Firmament*
Nadia Bou Ali, *Social Hell: Notes on the Undead in the Arrested Time of Genocide*
Dionne Brand, various poems and *Salvage: Readings from the Wreck*
Andrew Brooks, *Inferno*
Charlotte Brontë, *Jane Eyre*
Judith Butler, *Frames of War: When Is Life Grieveable?*
Joshua Clover, *Riot. Strike. Riot: The New Era of Uprisings*
Elias Doering (@f.shbone), various comics
Simone de Beauvoir, *The Second Sex*
Diane di Prima, *Revolutionary Letters*
Natalie Diaz, *Postcolonial Love Poem*
Omar El Akkad, *One Day Everyone Will Have Always Been Against This*
Mohammed El-Kurd, *Perfect Victims*
Frederick Engels, *The Principles of Communism*
Frantz Fanon, *The Wretched of the Earth*
Mark Fisher, *Capitalist Realism: Is There No Alternative?*
Édouard Glissant, *Poetics of Relation*
Elena Gomez, *Admit the Joyous Passion of Revolt*
Foie Gras (Iphigenia), various memes and graphics
Cricket Guest, video essays and *Final Girl Digital*
Ismatu Gwendolyn, *threadings.*
Christopher Hedges, *The Chris Hedges Report*
Noor Hindi, various poems
bell hooks, various essays and poems
Hasib Hourani, *Rock Flight*
Theron Harley Jacobs, *TPHD*
June Jordan, *The Essential June Jordan*
Bhanu Kapil, *Incubation: a space for monsters (2006/2023)*

Julia Kristeva, *Powers of Horror: An Essay on Abjection*
Spencer Krug, entire discography (especially as Moonface)
Audre Lorde, *Your Silence Will Not Protect You*
@luvicle, various memes and collage works
Momtaza Mehri, *Bad Diaspora Poems*
China Miéville, *A Spectre, Haunting: On the Communist Manifesto*
Mitski, all of it, on repeat
Aileen Moreton-Robinson, *Talkin' Up to the White Woman*
Gareth Morgan, *When a Punk Becomes a Spunk*
Eileen Myles (ed.), *Pathetic Literature*
Mary Oliver, all of it
Michael Ondaatje, *Collected Works of Billy the Kid*
Bisan Owda, *It's Bisan from Gaza and I'm Still Alive*
Claudia Rankine, *Citizen: An American Lyric*
Harry Reid, *Leave Me Alone*
Gillian Rose, *Love's Work* and *When Mourning Becomes the Law*
Jacqueline Rose, *Mothers: An Essay on Love and Cruelty*
Dasia Sade, *The Tragic Optimist's Guide to Surviving Capitalistic Nihilism*
Micaela Sahhar, *An Inventory of What I Do Not Wish to Write and of Which I Must Still Catalogue*
Edward Said, *Culture and Imperialism*
Elliot Sang, *Solidarity Is Supposed to Be Hard*
Eve Kosofsky Sedgwick, various writings
Charlotte Shane, *Meant for You*
Christina Sharpe, *Ordinary Notes*
Danez Smith, various poems
Susan Sontag, *Against Interpretation and Other Essays*
Keston Sutherland, *Meditations,* various essays and public talks, also personal correspondence
Joelle Taylor, *C+nto & Othered Poems*
Peyton Thomas, Notes on *Feral*

Brad Troemel, various video essays
Eve Tuck, various books, essays and talks but especially *Suspending Damage: A Letter to Communities, A Glossary of Haunting* (with C Ree) and *R Words: Refusing Research* (with K Wayne Yang)
Tiqqun, *Preliminary Materials for a Theory of the Young-Girl*
Jia Tolentino, *Trick Mirror*
Sofia Tolstoy (trans. Cathy Porter), *The Diaries of Sofia Tolstoy*
Lucy Van, *The Open*
Sam Wallman, *12 Rules for Strife*
We're In Hell, *The Internet Is All Over*

This collection's epigraph quotes Michael Ondaatje's 'Elimination Dance (An Intermission)' from *The Cinnamon Peeler: Selected Poems.* The opening untitled poem of 'NOTES ON ROTTING' ends with a line from Geoffrey Chaucer's *The Canterbury Tales,* as quoted in 'Elimination Dance (An Intermission)'.

The '256GB OF SALVAGED MEMORY' sequence responds to a composite of several personal digital archives and is significantly influenced by Cricket Guest's writings on girlhood and digital culture. '(i) 256GB OF SALVAGED MEMORY' quotes Scherezade Siobhan's poem 'querido', and Tiqqun's *Preliminary Materials for a Theory of the Young-Girl.* '(ii) 256GB OF SALVAGED MEMORY' quotes Mitski's song 'Class of 2013' from the album *Retired from Sad, New Career in Business.* '(iii) 256GB OF SALVAGED MEMORY' quotes Note 234 of Christina Sharpe's *Ordinary Notes* and Diana di Prima's 'Revolutionary Letter #96 Poem at Dawn'.

'On Desire' and the 'Long Future' sequence are directly engaged with Eve Tuck's body of work on desire, refusal, haunting and Indigenous research. 'On Desire' quotes Frederic Jameson's *The Political Unconscious*, Tuck's *Suspending Damage: A Letter to Communities* and Tuck and K Wayne Yang's *R-Words: Refusing Research*. 'i. Long Future' quotes a 2015 lecture for the Public Engagement and the Politics of Evidence in an Age of Neoliberalism and Audit Culture Symposium at University of Regina, 'Biting the Hand That Feeds You: Theories of Change in the Settler State and Its Universities'; a 2022 talk 'Decolonizing Place: A Conversation with Eve Tuck' hosted by the Clement A Price Institute; and Alicia Elliott's essay 'A Mind Spread Out on the Ground' from *Shapes of Native Non-Fiction*.

The 'On Ghosts' sequence is a response to Charlotte Brontë's novel *Jane Eyre*, and Cary Joji Fukunaga's 2011 film adaptation. 'i. On Ghosts' quotes Jude Ellison Sady Doyle's *Dead Blondes and Sad Mothers*, Kristin Chang's poem 'churching' and the essay 'The Carnivorous Nature of Girlhood' by Cricket Guest.

The 'Night Cries' sequence is a response to Tracey Moffatt's short film *Night Cries: A Rural Tragedy*, Charles Chauvel's *Jedda*, and Rosalie Kunoth Monk's 2014 *I am not the problem* speech on Q&A. 'ii. Night Cries' quotes Marcia Langton's essay '"Well, I Heard It on the Radio and Saw It on the Television": An essay for the Australian Film Commission on the politics and aesthetics of filmmaking by and about Aboriginal people and things.'

'iii. hip' quotes lyrics from Spencer Krug's song 'How We Have to Live', from the album *Twenty Twenty Twenty Twenty One.*

'Analysis Act One' quotes Noor Hindi's poem 'Fuck Your Lecture on Craft, My People Are Dying'. 'Analysis Act Two' references and quotes the essay 'Grand Unified Theory of Female Pain' by Leslie Jamison and James Baldwin's remarks from a 1984 interview with *The Paris Review.* 'Analysis Act Three' references JH Prynne's 2009 lecture for the Poem Presents Series at the University of Chicago, and lines from Keston Sutherland's 2017 collection *Whither Russia.*

'Losing Dogs' is a response to Mitski's song 'I Bet on Losing Dogs' from the album *Puberty 2.*

'I'm summoning Sofia Tolstoy from the bath with a spell I bought off Etsy' quotes passages from Sofia Tolstoy's diaries, as translated by Cathy Porter.

Acknowledgements

This work is deeply marked by so many different forms of love and relation.

I pay my respects, honour and grief to the Elders and teachers I've lost these last few years. Aunty Gloria Matthews, Uncle Wes Marne, Uncle Greg Simms and Drew Roberts – this is a darker world without you. I thank you for everything you did to light the path.

As always, I'm so privileged by the love and support of my family. You continue to shape me and the world around us with passion, integrity and joy. Being your daughter, sister, aunty and cousin means I will never abandon the task of building a better world. Giuseppe, Arabella, Theodore, Oliver, Aubrey, Ira, Teddy, Scarlett, you're always in aunty's mind and heart. Ebony and Zahra, I've loved being part of your family so much: you bring so much precious brightness and chaos to my life. To the Wilin mob – Tiriki, Leah, Kayla, Laniyuk, MJ, Narida, Kiara, Sal, Jodie, Rhea – you all make wage labour in the colony somehow nourishing. I don't know how I ever survived without you. Natasha, Giovanni, Elena, Emma, Paul, Natalie, Nayuka, Crystal, Jordy, Lina, Liz, Roxy, Mary – you all make the unpaid work and cancellations feel worth it. Ursula, thank you for your edits and our silly little girl dinners. Leah, thank you for your consolation and contextualisation of the enraging things we encounter in the world. Aiva and Edith, you're going to be okay, you're going to be so brilliant. Lakorra, Yileen and Ninda, you all already knew you're going to be fine (Raik, I will say something nice about you when you're old enough to read). Aunty Jeanine, Mykaela, Aunty Melissa, Lay, you are such lights in my sky. Aunty Alexis, Michelle, Jenn, John, thank you so much for your kind words of support – I admire you so much. Keston, our yarns made me a better poet and a better Marxist, and I'm so grateful for them. Sara, Nadine, Micaela, Hasib, Randa, Tasnim – I cherish every moment of instruction, leadership and guidance you've shared amidst your own horrific grief and the work you do to survive. I listen to you and I know we will see a free Palestine in our lives. Aviva and Yasmin, thank you for your persistence and dedication to this work that has slowly and stintingly spluttered into being.

This book wouldn't exist if Chloe Mills hadn't told me to write it the day I was heckled at Adelaide Writers' Week. I promised I'd write the book if she applied for the publicity job that meant we could work on this together, and I've been so honoured to share so much of this journey with her. Chloe is in so many of these poems, and a part of my being forever. This book wouldn't exist if Chloe didn't love, cherish and celebrate her friends and family with the generosity and care that she does. Chloe draws so much of that love from Grace, so I thank her, too.

In most ways this is a book for girls, but a girl is so many things. Everything, really. I've been honoured by the stories and feelings readers have shared with me over the past few years: I'm sorry if I was ever weird about it – I'm more frightened of you than you are of me. It has been a strange and humbling experience to hear what my work has meant to you. I hope you work towards a life where the grief of this book is just a shadow in your brighter world. I hope you tear down the violent infrastructure that has alienated us from the land, from each other, from ourselves.

And always, and of course, Jonathan, my love, my editor, my complete and utter life: there's nothing of this that I am or could ever be that doesn't know the warmth of your touch. Every word.